Alif Baa
with Multimedia
Introduction to Arabic
Letters and Sounds

Second Edition

ألف باء
مدخل الى
حروف العربية وأصواتها

الطبعة الثانية
مع Multimedia

Kristen Brustad   *Mahmoud Al-Batal*   *Abbas Al-Tonsi*

كرستن بروستاد   محمود البطل   عبّاس التونسي

Georgetown University Press
Washington D.C.

The production of the first edition of this textbook was supported by a grant from the National Endowment for the Humanities, an independent federal agency.

As of January 1, 2007, 13-digit ISBN numbers have replaced the 10-digit system.
13-digit   10-digit
   Paperback: 978-1-58901-506-7   Paperback: 1-58901-506-1

Georgetown University Press, Washington, D.C. www.press.georgetown.edu

Library of Congress Cataloging-in-Publication Data

Brustad, Kristen.
   Alif baa with Multimedia : introduction to Arabic letters and sounds / Kristen Brustad, Mahmoud Al-Batal, Abbas Al-Tonsi = Alife bā' : madkhal ilá hurūf al-'Arābīyah waaswatihā / Kristin Brūstād, Mahmūd al-Batal, 'Abbās al-Tūnisī. – 2nd ed.
         p. cm.
System requirements: System requirements for accompanying DVDs: PC; Windows 2000 or later; CD-ROM or DVD drive; Adobe Acrobat Reader; headphones or speakers; audio or video card.
Originally issued as: Alif Baa with DVDs, 2nd ed.; later ed. includes the same text and all of the audio and video on the disk as the earlier ed., except the format of the disk has been upgraded.
Includes bibliographical references and index.
ISBN 978-1-58901-506-7 (pbk. : alk. paper)
   1. Arabic language—Writing. 2. Arabic language—Phonetics. 3. Arabic language—Textbooks for foreign speakers—English. I. Title: Alif bā'. II. Al-Batal, Mahmoud. III. Tūnisī, 'Abbās. IV. Title.
PJ6123.B78 2009
492.781'3—dc22   2009007016

This book is printed on acid-free paper meeting the requirements of the American National Standard for Permanence in Paper for Printed Library Materials.

15 14 13 12 11 10 09   9 8 7 6

Printed in the United States of America

TABLE OF CONTENTS

		Page
Preface: To the Student		vii
To the Teacher		ix
Acknowledgments		xi
Introduction: The Arabic Alphabet		1
Unit One: الوحدة الأولى Unit One		9
ا	*aa (alif)*	9
ب	*baa*	11
ت	*taa*	13
ث	<u>*th*</u>*aa*	15
و	*uu*	17
ي	*ii*	18
Vowel Length		20
ـَ	*a (fatHa)*	21
ـُ	*u (Damma)*	22
ـِ	*i (kasra)*	23
Vocabulary		25
Culture: Saying Hello		26
Arabic Dialects		26
Unit Two: الوحدة الثانية		28
ج	*jiim (giim)*	28
ح	*Haa*	31
خ	*khaa*	33
ـْ	*sukuun*	35
و	*waaw*	36
ي	*yaa*	37
Vocabulary		38
Culture: *HaDritik, HaDritak*		39

Unit Three: الوحدة الثالثة   **40**

     أ   *hamza* 40

     د   *daal* 43

     ذ   <u>*dh*</u>*aal* 44

     ر   *raa* 46

     ز   *zaay* 47

     Culture: Meeting and Greeting People 49

           al-Hamdu lillaah 49

     Vocabulary 50

Unit Four: الوحدة الرابعة   **51**

     ّ   *shadda* 51

     س   *siin* 54

     ش   <u>*sh*</u>*iin* 56

     ص   *Saad* 58

     ض   *Daad* 61

     Vocabulary 65

     Gender 66

Unit Five: الوحدة الخامسة   **67**

     ة   *taa marbuuTa* 67

     ط   *Taa* 69

     ظ   <u>*DH*</u>*aa* 72

     ع   ^c*ayn* 75

     غ   <u>*gh*</u>*ayn* 78

     Vocabulary 82

     Culture: *Forms of Address* 85

Unit Six: الوحدة السادسة **86**

 ف   *faa* **86**

 ق   *qaaf* **88**

 ك   *kaaf* **90**

 ل   *laam* **94**

 Expressions with الله **95**

 لا   *laam alif* **97**

 Vocabulary **99**

 Culture: اتفضّل/اتفضّلي **102**

Unit Seven: الوحدة السابعة   **103**

 م   *miim* **103**

 ن   *nuun* **107**

 هـ   *haa* **109**

 Alphabet Chart **114**

 Arabic Numerals and Numbers (1-10) **115**

 Vocabulary **118**

 Culture: Coffee Time! **120**

Unit Eight: الوحدة الثامنة   **121**

 الـ   ألف لام **121**

 أ   همزة الوَصل **125**

 ٰ   dagger alif **127**

 Vocabulary **128**

 Culture: سَلامتك! **130**

      مَعلِهْش! **130**

Unit Nine: الوحدة التاسعة   **131**

 ى   ألف مَقصورة **131**

 آ   ألف مَدَّة **133**

 ئ   همزة على كرسي الياء **134**

 ؤ   همزة على كرسي الواو **135**

 Vocabulary **136**

 Culture: Visiting People **140**

Unit Ten: الوحدة العاشرة   **141**

تنوين 141

تَنوين الفَتح ـً   142

تَنوين الضَمّ ـٌ   143

تَنوين الكَسر ـٍ   144

Writing One-Letter Particles: بِـ لِـ و 147

Justification of Margins 148

Handwriting 148

Culture: The Development of the Arabic Writing System 150

Calligraphy 151

Appendix: Texts of the Egyptian Colloquial Dialogues
on the Accompanying DVDs 152

English-Arabic Glossary 159

PREFACE

To the Student

Ahlan wa Sahlan! Welcome to Arabic! This textbook, *Alif Baa*, represents the first in a series of textbooks aimed at teaching Arabic to English-speaking students, followed by *Al-Kitaab fii Ta^callum al-^cArabiyya I, II,* and *III.*

The present book aims to help you learn to pronounce the sounds of Arabic and write its letters, and to introduce to you a number of greetings, common phrases, and basic vocabulary, as well as aspects of Arab culture. The book is accompanied by two DVDs for you to use outside of class. You will find most of the listening exercises and writing drills in this book on these DVDs in interactive format that lets you click on letters and words to hear them. This new edition of *Alif Baa* also includes visual footage of a calligrapher writing the letters so that you have a model to follow as you work through them.

The book consists of an introduction, ten units, an appendix and an English-Arabic Glossary. The introduction provides a brief overview of some special characteristics of Arabic, and the ten units present the alphabet in groups following the modern Arabic order, with the exception that all of the long vowels are presented in the first unit. In describing the sounds, we have avoided technical descriptions, opting instead for a more practical approach involving tips and exercises that focus on the points of articulation of the sounds. Following the description of each sound, we have provided a brief explanation of the writing of the corresponding letter. Each unit contains a number of recorded listening exercises and drills on reading, writing, connecting letters, and dictation. We have used only meaningful words in these exercises, because word structure in Arabic is based on consonant-vowel patterns, and listening to a large number of words, even if you do not know their meaning, will help you begin internalizing these patterns and facilitate learning vocabulary. We do not expect you to learn these words; their purpose is merely to illustrate sounds and word patterns. The vocabulary that you are expected to learn is in a separate section on the DVD and at the end of each unit. We have also included in this book examples of authentic or "real-life" Arabic from newspapers, books, and magazines, and on the DVD you will find pictures of Arabic signs from the streets of Morocco, Egypt, and Lebanon. Finally, we have included short cultural notes explaining some aspects of the situations that you will see on the DVD. The appendix provides the texts of all the dialogues on the DVD, and the glossary includes all the vocabulary items introduced in the book.

We believe that it is crucial for you to learn to recognize and produce Arabic sounds accurately from the outset, for several reasons. First, you must learn to pronounce Arabic correctly in order to communicate effectively with Arabic speakers. Second, Arabic sounds are not very difficult. Many non-native speakers have learned to pronounce Arabic sounds accurately, and there is no reason why you should not expect to do so as well. Third, it is important to learn the sounds correctly now when you have the time to concentrate on them; later you will be concentrating on other aspects of the language, such as vocabulary and grammar. Fourth, the structure of the Arabic language has at its core groups of consonant sounds that have meaning, so that the ability to recognize sounds accurately when you hear them will greatly enhance your ability to understand, learn, and remember vocabulary. Fifth, Arabic is largely phonetic, which means that if you learn the sounds correctly now, you will not suffer from spelling headaches. Finally, we do not agree with the commonly

held assumption that Arabic is too difficult for non-native speakers to learn: all languages require a certain amount of exposure, time, and effort, and the ability to learn a foreign language is directly related to both the desire to do so and the belief that you can.

Tips for Using This Book:

1. Prepare for active participation in class. To do this you need to spend time outside of class listening to and working with the DVD exercises. Listen to and write the new sounds and letters as many times as you need to in order to feel comfortable recognizing and producing them. Prepare the lesson assigned beforehand, so that you will be ready to read and write. Class time should be spent practicing, not listening to lectures.

2. Once is not enough. Whether you are pronouncing new sounds, writing new letters, or studying vocabulary, you should repeat the activity as many times as you can. Repeat until you can produce a sound or write a letter easily. Remember that you are training your brain and your muscles to do new things, and this takes practice. Listen to the DVDs as many times as you can, and go back over items that you missed on the homework. Although most of your studies are visually oriented, you learned your native language mainly through hearing and listening, and not through reading and writing. Rediscover your native ability to learn through listening by devoting as much time as you can while working through this book to the listening and dictation exercises.

3. Study out loud. The only way to train your brain and your mouth to speak this language is by doing—thinking about it is not enough! Practice speaking at every chance you get. **Talk to your classmates and others, and talk to yourself.**

4. Study in groups. You are much more likely to study **actively** when you study with others. Good group activities include quizzing and dictating to each other, and making up sentences and dialogues.

5. Review constantly. Set aside part of your study time each day to go over old material and practice sounds and letters you learned previously. This investment will pay off in improved accuracy in listening, speaking, reading and writing. Reviewing old material will make it stick, and will help you refine your writing and pronunciation.

6. Expect to feel tired occasionally. Being tired is a good sign—it means that you are concentrating, and that you are training your muscles to produce new sounds correctly. Remember that you will soon be able to do easily things that tire you at first.

We wish you a successful and enjoyable learning experience!

To the Teacher

This textbook, and the continuing books in the *Al-Kitaab* series, are constructed around a philosophy of teaching and learning Arabic that has developed, and continues to develop, over more than sixty years of combined experience. We ask that you, the instructor, read this preface as well as the Preface to the Student, and that you have your students read the latter, so that everyone understands the principles underlying the structure and contents of these materials.

First and most importantly, these materials are designed so that students can do most of the preparation and actual learning of new material outside of class, in order for class time to be spent doing exercises, watching and practicing conversations, and working *with* Arabic (instead of hearing *about* it). In this second edition, students have available to them on DVD (in addition to all of the material that was on tape or CD in the first edition) visual footage of a calligrapher writing all the letters of the alphabet, and new versions of the colloquial dialogues, whose texts are found in the Appendix. We believe that it is crucial to expect a high degree of effort from students in preparing for class, and equally, that this effort must be rewarded by spending class time doing activities that permit maximum participation by all students. Since the book is designed so that the students can do much of their learning outside of class, each person may work at his or her own pace, so that differences in learning speed need not affect the class as a whole. It is also important that students realize right away that the burden of learning is on them, because this helps them to become active learners. Finally, it is essential to follow through on the expectations you set. Do not reward students who have not prepared, and punish those who have, by "teaching" them what they should have done outside of class.

Second, it is our conviction that everyone can produce Arabic sounds accurately, and that it is necessary to encourage and even to expect accuracy from the outset. Not only is this the only opportunity you and the students will have to focus all of your attention on the phonetic aspects of Arabic, it is also better to form good habits from the start. We believe all language skills to be important, and that they reinforce each other. The ability to hear the difference between, for example, ك and ق is a necessary prelude to being able to produce them, and the ability to do both will aid in mastering Arabic morphology, the root and pattern system, spelling, and retaining vocabulary.

Third, the inclusion of dialogues in colloquial Arabic represents a fundamental aspect of our teaching philosophy, which views Arabic as one language, albeit one rich in registers and varieties. Since each register of Arabic reflects vital parts of Arab culture, students need to learn formal and informal varieties to understand both the language and the culture. Our decision to include an introduction to colloquial Arabic was also a natural consequence of our desire to use language forms appropriate to context. It is the goal of this textbook series to provide a framework for introducing students to both registers while focusing on the formal and leaving as much flexibility to the teacher as possible. The extent to which you emphasize each variety will depend on your program and the needs of your students. We have found through experience that this approach does not confuse students as long as spoken variants are introduced as individual vocabulary items and expressions. On the contrary, exposure to colloquial greetings and expressions adds to their pool of vocabulary, and, more importantly, gives them the tools they need to begin communicating with native speakers they might meet or know in their immediate environment, who will not speak to them in formal Arabic.

The accompanying DVDs contain twelve dialogues that were filmed in Egypt in the Cairene dialect. We decided to use the dialect of Cairo in this edition of the materials because it is the most widely understood among Arabic speakers. However, it is not our desire to impose the teaching of the Egyptian dialect on anyone; if your own dialect differs, we encourage you to teach your students the forms with which you are comfortable. (You can use the visual content and create your own voice over.) The students have these dialogues on their DVDs so that they can watch them on their own, but they will need your help in understanding the content of these dialogues, since we have not introduced the colloquial vocabulary in the book. It is not our goal for the students to write out the dialogues. On the contrary: it is good training for the students to develop confidence in their aural and oral skills at this stage, and they need to be encouraged to rely on their "phonographic" rather than their "photographic" memory. Everyone has natural aural and oral language learning skills; no one learned her or his native language through reading.

While we have included short cultural notes in the book meant to accompany the video scenes, we have not provided detailed lesson plans in order to give you the flexibility to proceed as you wish and focus on the aspects you deem important. Use the DVDs and cultural notes as starting points, encourage questions and discussion, and expand as you wish. We suggest that you have the students listen to each dialogue several times as follows: (1) Before explaining anything, have them watch for general content, then ask what they understood. (2) Have them watch again, as many times as necessary, to listen for individual words or expressions, followed by discussion and explanation of what they heard. (3) Have them watch a final time, after they have understood *what* is said, to focus on *how* it is said. After that, the students should be ready to try out the expressions themselves, so let them make up their own situations and act them out. Your own contribution will be vital to the success of these materials.

The material in this textbook can be covered well in twenty- to twenty-five contact hours, depending on the amount of time devoted to the various activities, assuming class time is not spent on lectures, and that students will devote one to two hours a night to doing the drills. All the exercises in the textbook except the reading ones are meant to be done as homework. Spend as much class time as possible on activities involving speaking, dictation, and reading aloud. This approach stresses dictation because we believe that the mastery of sounds and the ability to relate sounds and writing must be developed early. Repeat sounds and words many times over, and have students repeat as a group to take the pressure off individual performance. It takes several repetitions of a new or unfamiliar sound in order to identify it, and several more to be able to produce it.

Each unit also includes a vocabulary section so that students may begin to acquire an active vocabulary. Playing games is a good way to help them activate these words. In addition, we encourage you to begin teaching students a few common verbs (such as *study, live, drink, eat*) so that they can interact with each other in Arabic. It is not necessary for them to get the whole conjugation; first and second person singular forms are enough for them to begin talking to each other. Introducing words that the students will get in *Al-Kitaab*, or whatever textbook you use, will smooth the transition into the next stage.

Also included in most units is a section called Arabic Signs, which consists of street and shop signs filmed in Morocco, Egypt, and Lebanon. Reading these in small groups in class is a fun activity that gives them linguistic as well as cultural exposure.

Of course, no textbook can take the place of a good teacher. It is our hope that these materials will help you to enrich your classroom and make learning Arabic an enjoyable experience for your students.

ACKNOWLEDGMENTS

PRODUCTION OF DVDs BY MULTIMEDIA COMPANY, MOHAMMED SHAHEEN, DIRECTOR
PRODUCTION OF COLLOQUIAL DIALOGUES BY NASHWA MOHSIN ZAYID
ARABIC CALLIGRAPHY BY PROFESSOR SAYYID EL-SHINNAWI, ZAYID UNIVERSITY, U.A.E.
DRAWINGS BY ANNE MARIE SKYE, WWW.AMSKYEART.COM

We would like to express our deep gratitude to all the institutions and individuals who made the production of this book possible. The National Endowment for the Humanities provided the funding for the first edition of the textbook through a grant to the School of Arabic at Middlebury College, and Middlebury College provided matching funds and staff support. The Emory College Language Center and its staff, Jose Rodriguez, Johnny Waggener, and student assistant Khaled Krisht, provided invaluable technical assistance during all phases of producing the second edition. Thanks are also due to Melanie Clouser, who proofread the manuscript and made valuable suggestions.

The difficult and tedious job of producing the DVDs was superbly carried out by the Multimedia Company in Cairo, directed by Mohammed Shaheen. A number of talented and dedicated people worked and patiently reworked everything from sounds to the screen fonts to meet our demand to make everything as clear and sharp as humanly possible. Their creativity and professionalism are clearly evident in the final product.

A special acknowledgment is also due to producer Nashwa Mohsin Zayid and the cinematography team she assembled. The director, actors, camera and sound professionals worked extremely long hours to create the colloquial dialogues scenes in the accompanying DVDs. The extra effort they put into filming and editing have resulted in the product you now have, the quality of which speaks for itself.

We are very grateful to Anne Marie Skye and Professor Sayyid El-Shinnawi for their beautiful artistic additions to the materials. Their drawings and calligraphy have made a big difference not only in the aesthetic quality of the new edition, but also its educational value.

Alf shukr to our colleagues Housni Bennis, Ikram Masmoudi, Olla Al-Shalchi, Awad Mubarak, Shukri Gohar, and Wafa Abouneaj for their beautiful video introductions.

Our colleagues at Georgetown University Press were instrumental in helping us realize the ambitious additions to this second edition of *Alif Baa*. Special thanks go to Richard Brown, director, and Gail Grella, associate director and acquisitions editor, for continued support of the project. We are grateful to the entire staff for their dedicated and careful work in producing these materials.

Last but not least, we thank all the students and colleagues who used the first edition of the book and took the trouble to write us with suggestions for improvements. We have tried to incorporate as many as possible. We hope that the new edition will prove to be more helpful to students and teachers alike.

مع خالص الشكر والتقدير لكم جميعاً!

INTRODUCTION
THE ARABIC ALPHABET

The Arabic alphabet contains twenty-eight letters consisting of consonants and long vowels, and fourteen symbols that function as short vowels and pronunciation markers, or as markers of certain grammatical functions. Units One through Ten will introduce these letters and symbols individually.

First, take a look at the alphabet in the chart below, which shows the twenty-eight letters. Starting in the upper right-hand corner, the chart reads across from right to left, which is the direction Arabic is written and read. To see and hear the pronunciation of these letters, click on each box on your DVD screen.

DVD The DVD symbol indicates that you should listen to/watch the DVD.

ث	ت	ب	ا
د	خ	ح	ج
س	ز	ر	ذ
ط	ض	ص	ش
ف	غ	ع	ظ
م	ل	ك	ق
ي	و	هـ	ن

The next chart shows the fourteen extra-alphabetical symbols and their names. They include short vowels, pronunciation symbols, grammatical endings, spelling variants, and a consonant that, for historical reasons, is not represented in the alphabet chart. These symbols will be introduced in Units One through Ten along with the alphabet.

‑ٖ kasra	‑ُ Damma	‑َ fatHa
‑ّ shadda	ء hamza	‑ْ sukuun
‑ٰ dagger alif	أ waSla	ة taa marbuuTa
	آ madda	ى alif maqSuura
‑ٍ tanwiin al-kasr	‑ٌ tanwiin aD-Damm	‑ً tanwiin al-fatH

SPECIAL CHARACTERISTICS OF THE ARABIC SCRIPT

The Arabic alphabet and writing system has four major characteristics that distinguish it from its European counterparts.

1. Arabic is written from right to left. One consequence of this ordering system is that Arabic books, newspapers, and magazines open and are read in the opposite direction from European and American printed materials.

2. Letters are connected in both print and handwriting, unlike those of the Latin alphabet, which are connected only in handwriting. The following are individual letters which are written one after the other in correct order, but which do not form a word written this way:

ا ل ب ا ب

When they are connected, however, they do spell a word: البــاب ("al-baab" *the door*).

Notice that not all the letters in الباب connect to the following letter. This is a characteristic of certain letters that you will master as you learn to write. See if you can identify the nonconnecting letters in the following words:

مبارك   أسد   زين   السودان   لذيذ

As you learn the alphabet, note which letters connect and which do not, and when you write words, do not lift the pen or pencil from the page until you get to a natural break with a nonconnecting letter.

3. **Letters have slightly different shapes** depending on where they occur in a word. The chart on page 1 gives the forms of the letters when written independently; these forms vary when the letters are written in initial, medial, and final position. "Initial position" means not connected to a previous letter, "medial position" indicates that the letter is between two other letters, and "final position" means connected to the preceding letter. Most letters have a particularly distinct shape when they occur in final position, similar to the way English can have capital letters at the beginning of words. The chart below gives you an idea of the extent of this variation. You will see that each letter retains a basic shape throughout; this is the core of the letter. If the letter has dots, their number and position also remain the same. Note that the last three letters, which all connect, appear to have a "tail" in their independent and final forms which drops off when they are connected and is replaced by a connecting segment that rests on the line. Try to find the core shape of each letter, its dots, if any, the connecting segments, and the final tail in the following chart.

Final Position	Medial Position	Initial Position	Independent Shape
ل	ل	ا	ا
ـث	ـثـ	ثـ	ث
ـج	ـجـ	جـ	ج
ـع	ـعـ	عـ	ع

As you learn each letter of the alphabet, you will learn to read and write all its various shapes. You will be surprised how quickly you master them, with a little practice!

4. Arabic script consists of two separate "layers" of writing. The basic skeleton of a word is made up of the consonants and long vowels. Short vowels and other pronunciation and grammatical markers are separated from the consonant skeleton of the word. This second layer, called vocalization, is normally omitted in writing, and the reader recognizes words without it. Compare the following two versions of the same text, a line of poetry, the first of which represents the normal way of writing, without vocalization, and the second of which has all the pronunciation markers added:

بسقط اللوى بين الدخول فحومل   قفا نبك من ذكرى حبيب ومنزل

بِسِقْطِ ٱللِّوَى بَيْنَ ٱلدَّخُولِ فَحَوْمَلِ   قِفَا نَبْكِ مِنْ ذِكْرَى حَبِيبٍ وَمَنْزِلِ

من معلقة امرئ القيس

Texts normally vocalized include elementary school textbooks, some editions of classical literary texts, and religious texts such as the Quran and the Bible. In the scriptures, this precision has religious significance: the extra markings on the text leave no doubt as to the exact reading intended. Thus the texts of the Quran and Bible show full vocalization, as you can see in the following excerpts.

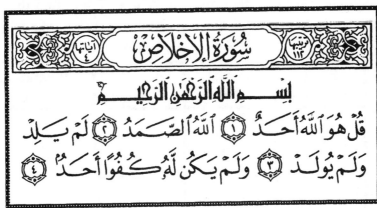

من القرآن الكريم سورة الإخلاص

البدء

١   فِي ٱلْبَدْءِ خَلَقَ ٱللَّهُ ٱلسَّمَاوَاتِ وَٱلْأَرْضَ . وَكَانَتِ ٱلْأَرْضُ خَرِبَةً وَخَالِيَةً ، وَعَلَى وَجْهِ ٱلْغَمْرِ ظُلْمَةٌ ، وَرُوحُ ٱللَّهِ يَرِفُّ عَلَى وَجْهِ ٱلْمِيَاهِ . وَقَالَ ٱللَّهُ : «لِيَكُنْ نُورٌ» ، فَكَانَ نُورٌ . وَرَأَى ٱللَّهُ ٱلنُّورَ أَنَّهُ حَسَنٌ . وَفَصَلَ ٱللَّهُ بَيْنَ ٱلنُّورِ وَٱلظُّلْمَةِ . وَدَعَا ٱللَّهُ ٱلنُّورَ نَهَاراً ، وَٱلظُّلْمَةُ دَعَاهَا لَيْلاً .

من الكتاب المقدس ، سفر التكوين

- 4 -

In schoolbooks, vowel markings are used to introduce new vocabulary and to enable the students to learn the correct pronunciation of formal Arabic with all the correct grammatical endings. The following example is taken from a Syrian fourth-grade elementary reader.

كَرَمٌ عَرَبِيٌّ

في قَديمِ الزَّمانِ ، مَرَّتْ بالجَزيرَةِ العَرَبِيَّةِ سَنَةُ مَحْلٍ قاسِيَةٌ ، فَلا مَطَرَ تَسْخُو بِهِ السَّماءُ ، وَلا زَرْعَ تَجُودُ بِهِ الأَرْضُ ؛ فَعَمَّ البُؤْسُ ، واشْتَدَّتِ الحاجَةُ إلى الطَّعامِ . كانَ كُرَماءُ العَرَبِ يُساعِدُونَ المُحْتاجِينَ ، وكانَ مِنْ أكْرَمِهِمْ حاتِمٌ الطَّائِيُّ .

من كتاب القراءة للصف الرابع الابتدائي ، ج. ٢، وزارة التربية السورية، ١٩٨٦

Thereafter, the students see the words in regular, unvocalized script. You will learn vocabulary the same way.

Most books, magazines, and newspapers are unvocalized, as the following newspaper article demonstrates.

فيدوفين في بيروت

وصل إلى بيروت، بعد ظهر أمس، الموفد الخاص لوزير خارجية الاتحاد الروسي لمنطقة الشرق الأوسط اندريه فيدوفين، آتياً من القاهرة، للقاء المسؤولين اللبنانيين والبحث معهم في تطورات الأوضاع في لبنان والمنطقة. وكان في استقباله في المطار السفير الروسي بوريس بولوتين.

من جريدة الحياة، يونيو (حزيران) ٢٠٠٣

In unvocalized texts, possible ambiguities in form occasionally arise; however, rarely does this result in ambiguous meaning.

In this textbook series, vocalization marks will be used when new vocabulary is introduced, but thereafter you will be expected to have memorized the pronunciation of the word, and these marks will be omitted. Since Arabic speakers normally read and write without vocalization, it is best to become accustomed to reading and writing that way from the beginning.

جامعة وِشكنسِن

يَدُ المَلِك يَدُ مَلِك

PRONUNCIATION OF ARABIC

In addition to the characteristics of the Arabic script, you should also be aware of certain features of the sounds of Arabic.

1. Arabic has a one-to-one correspondence between sound and letter, whereas English spelling often uses one letter or combination of letters to represent several different sounds. Consider the plural marker *s* in the words *dogs* and *books*, and note that the sound of the first is actually *z*, not *s*. Compare also the two different sounds spelled as *th* as in *think* and *those*. These are two distinct sounds, and Arabic has two different letters to represent them. American English speakers sometimes confuse pronunciation and spelling without realizing it. For example, think about the word *television*. This word has been adopted into Arabic and is pronounced something like *tilivizyoon*. It is also spelled with the Arabic letter that corresponds to the sound *z*, because that is the way it is pronounced. English spelling, on the other hand, requires an *s*, even though there is no *s* sound in the word. Pay attention to the sounds of the Arabic letters, and avoid associating English letters with them.

2. The Arabic writing system is regularly phonetic, which means that words are generally written as they are pronounced. Learn to recognize and pronounce the sounds correctly now, and not only will you avoid spelling problems, but you will also learn and retain vocabulary more easily.

3. In general, Arabic sounds use a wider range of mouth and throat positions than English. Be aware of what parts of the mouth you must use to produce these sounds properly from the beginning, when you are able to focus the most attention on them. You will learn to make new sounds, and to do so, you must become familiar with a set of muscles that you use to make sounds like gargling or coughing but not to speak English. Your muscles are capable of making all these sounds, but you need to become conscious of what they are doing and you must practice. Just as you must train your arm to hit a tennis ball, you must train your throat to contract or tighten, and this takes constant repetition. As you keep your eye on the ball in tennis, keep your mind on the sounds you are making at all times. With practice, you will be able to do this with less and less effort.

A NOTE ON TRANSLITERATION

While you are learning the alphabet, you will need a system of transliteration, or way of representing Arabic sounds and words in the Latin alphabet. We have devised a simplified system for use in these materials that we use when necessary; that is, when we cannot write the Arabic symbols because you do not know them yet, or when the page layout of the book makes it difficult or impossible. We recommend you learn and use this system unless you are a trained linguist and have another system you prefer. However, using transliteration should be a temporary, transitional stage, and you should move to writing solely in Arabic as soon as possible. Do not let transliteration become a crutch.

The key to a good transliteration system is that each different sound should have its own unique symbol. It is not a good idea to just write Arabic words "the way they sound." You need to be listening for Arabic sounds as Arabic, without trying to approximate them to English sounds. Moreover, English spelling tends to be inconsistent, especially in its vowel sounds and spellings (think of how many different sounds *o* and *u* represent). The system used in these materials is given in the following chart. Note in particular the use of capital letters to represent emphatic sounds and double vowels to represent long vowels.

Transliteration Symbol	Arabic Sound
DH	ظ
c	ع
gh	غ
f	ف
q	ق
k	ك
l	ل
m	م
n	ن
h	ﻫ
uu/w	و
ii/y	ي
a	ـَ
u	ـُ
i	ـِ
'	ء

Transliteration Symbol	Arabic Sound
aa	ا
b	ب
t	ت
th	ث
j	ج
H	ح
kh	خ
d	د
dh	ذ
r	ر
z	ز
s	س
sh	ش
S	ص
D	ض
T	ط

UNITS ONE THROUGH TEN

In Units One through Ten, you will learn the basics of reading, writing, and speaking Arabic. Listen to the DVD as you read, make a habit of pronouncing *out loud* everything you write while you are writing it, and practice on your own in addition to doing the drills in the book. The more time you put in now, the easier it will be to learn vocabulary, pronounce and spell words correctly, and speak and read fluently.

يلّا بنا ! *yalla bina!* Let's go!

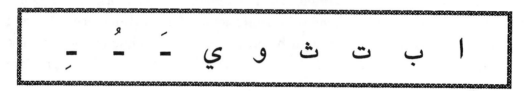

الوحدة الاولى
UNIT ONE

ا   ب   ت   ث   و   ي   ـَ   ـُ   ـِ

This unit will introduce you to the first four letters of the Arabic alphabet and to the long and short vowels.

ا

aa (alif)

The name of the first letter of the Arabic alphabet is *alif*. Alif has two main functions, the first of which will be introduced in this unit, and the second in Unit Three. Here we are concerned with its function as a long vowel, whose pronunciation resembles that of *a* in *bad* or in *father*. Say these two words aloud and notice the difference in the quality of the *a*: the former is pronounced in the front of the mouth, while the latter is deeper and farther back. The pronunciation of alif has a similar range; we will refer to these differences in pronunciation as **vowel quality**. Two factors influence the quality of alif: regional dialect and surrounding consonants.

In the eastern regions of the Arab world (the Arabian Peninsula, Iraq), the sound of alif is generally deeper, closer to *father*, while farther west, especially in North Africa, it tends to be frontal, closer to *bad* or even the sound of English *e* in words like *bet*. You will notice this regional variation when you interact with Arabic speakers from different countries.

The other reason for variation in the quality of alif is shared by all speakers, and has to do with surrounding consonants. Arabic has several "emphatic" consonant sounds that are pronounced farther back in the mouth, and these consonants deepen the sound of a neighboring alif so that it resembles *father*. Learning to discern and produce this difference in vowel quality will help you understand, speak, and write Arabic accurately. The following exercises will get you started, but remember to keep paying attention to vowel quality as you work through this book.

LISTENING EXERCISE 1. 📀
TO HEAR THE FRONTAL AND DEEP VARIANTS OF ALIF, LISTEN TO THE FOLLOWING PAIRS OF WORDS BY CLICKING ON THEM ON YOUR DVD. THE FIRST WORD IN EACH PAIR CONTAINS A FRONTAL ALIF THAT CONTRASTS WITH THE DEEP ALIF IN THE SECOND. LISTEN TO AND REPEAT THESE SOUNDS ALOUD SEVERAL TIMES, UNTIL YOU CAN HEAR THE DIFFERENCE CLEARLY AND PRODUCE IT.

تاب / طاب   ساح / صاح   داني / ضاني   ذال / ظالم

You may have noticed that the first word of each pair in Listening Exercise 1 begins with a familiar consonant sound, whereas the second word begins with a different sound that resembles the first but is pronounced with the tongue lower and farther back in the mouth. These latter sounds are often called "emphatic" consonants, and they affect the pronunciation of surrounding vowel sounds. Listening for the difference between frontal and deep alif is the best way to distinguish between emphatic and nonemphatic consonants. We will discuss this point in more depth later when you begin learning the emphatic letters.

DRILL 1. DVD

CLICK ON EACH NUMBER ON YOUR DVD AND YOU WILL HEAR A WORD. FOR EACH, NOTE WHETHER THE ALIF IS FRONTAL **(F)** OR DEEP **(D)**:

1. _____   4. _____   7. _____   10. _____

2. _____   5. _____   8. _____   11. _____

3. _____   6. _____   9. _____   12. _____

WRITING DVD

This box contains (from right to left) the independent, initial, medial, and final shapes of the letter alif.

In this section you will learn to write the various shapes of the letter alif. Watch Calligrapher Professor Sayyid El-Shinnawi write the shapes of alif on your DVD as you read and write this section. Learn to draw the letters using the same hand motions he does.

Alone or at the beginning of a word, the alif is written as a single stroke, drawn from top to bottom, as the arrow in the example shows. Practice on the blank lines below, copying the example on the first line, pronouncing alif as you write it as many times as you can in the space provided:

When the alif follows another letter, it is written from the bottom up. The previous letter will end in a connecting segment drawn on the line. Start with that segment, then draw the alif from the bottom up as shown:

In either case, **the alif does not connect to what follows it.** Always pick your pen up from the page after writing alif.

Now practice reading alif by circling all of the alifs you can find in the following sentence (taken from *1001 Nights*):

كان يا ما كان في قديم الزمان، كان تاجر كثير المال والاعمال . . .

baa

The second letter of the Arabic alphabet is pronounced like English *b*. This consonant lends vowels a frontal quality.

LISTENING EXERCISE 2. DVD

LISTEN TO AND REPEAT THE WORDS CONTAINING ب , FOCUSING ON THE FRONTAL QUALITY OF THE VOWELS.

حب   بيت   ليبيا   لبنان   باب   باء

WRITING DVD

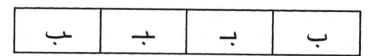

The independent, initial, medial, and final shapes of the letter baa have in common a "tooth" and a single dot below the line.

Watch Professor El-Shinnawi write the shapes of this letter on your DVD as you read and write this section. Unlike alif , this is a **connecting** letter, which means that it connects to any letter following it in the same word. The main parts of the letter, the initial tooth and the dot beneath the body, remain constant in all four shapes. Compare the independent and final shapes, and note that both end in a second tooth. Think of this tooth as the "tail" of the letter that occurs when it occurs at the end of a word. It is not written in initial and medial positions because the letter ب always connects to the following letter in those cases.

When written alone, this letter takes the shape shown in the rightmost box above. Following the steps shown in the example on the first line below, trace the letter with your pencil a few times, then write it. First, write the body: from right to left, begin with a small hook, then continue straight along the line and end with another hook for the tail. After you

have finished the body, place the dot below the letter as shown (you can associate the sound *b* with the dot *below* the letter).

ر͟͟ح ب ـب ①
② .

When followed by another letter, it connects to that letter by dropping the final hook: ـب . When writing this and other connecting dotted letters, you should place the dot more or less in vertical alignment with the initial tooth of the letter. The exact length of the body and placement of the dot may vary somewhat according to the style of the handwriting or print font; study the various styles you see and imitate the one that suits you.

ـب ①
② .

Now write the first two letters of the alphabet joined together: با . Do not pick up the pen to cross the ـب until you have finished writing the alif joined to it. Copy the example and pronounce it aloud:

با ا ①
② .

When ـبـ occurs in medial position, connecting segments link this letter to previous and following ones as shown. (This will become clearer when you learn a few more letters.) Copy the example:

ـبـ ①
② .

Final ـب resembles the independent form with the final hook. This form may be illustrated by writing two ب 's together: بب . Copy the example:

بـيـ بـ ①
③ ②

Now you can write your first word in Arabic: باب *door* . Practice writing this word by copying the example shown below, pronouncing it out loud as you write. **Remember:** do not stop to dot the letters until you have finished the skeletal structure of the entire word.

باب باب

ت

taa

The third letter of the alphabet is pronounced like a clear, frontal English *t*. How many different ways do you pronounce *t*? Read the following list aloud the way you would normally pronounce the words when speaking: *bottle, teeth, automatic*. Of these words, most American speakers pronounce the *t* in *teeth* farther forward in the mouth, against the back of the teeth. This is the correct position of the tongue for the pronunciation of this Arabic sound; do not confuse it with the flap of the tongue you use to produce *automatic*. Arabic ت must be pronounced with the tip of your tongue against your teeth, but without aspiration.[1] Since ت is a frontal letter, the vowel sounds surrounding it are frontal too; in particular, the alif and fatHa (short *a*) are pronounced like *a* in *bad* and *e* as in *bet* (**not** like *a* in *father* and *u* in *but*).

[1]Aspiration refers to the breathy sound often heard with *t*, *p*, and *k*. Light a match, hold it in front of your mouth, and say, *Peter, Tom, and Kirk went to town*. The flame will flicker each time you pronounce one of these letters. Arabic sounds do not have aspiration, so practice saying *t* and *k* with a lit match in front of your mouth until you can pronounce them without making the flame flicker.

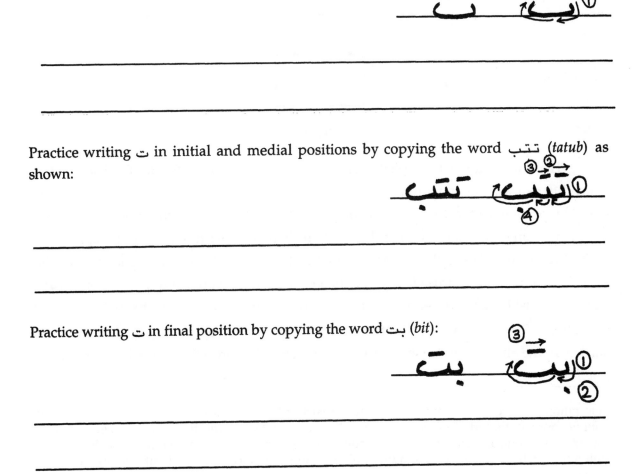

LISTEN TO THE SOUND OF THE LETTER ت AND REPEAT. PAY ATTENTION TO THE POSITION OF YOUR TONGUE AS YOU DO SO AND NOTICE THE FRONTAL QUALITY OF THE VOWELS.

شتاء   بنت   وتد   توت   بات   تاء

WRITING 📀

ـت	ـتـ	تـ	ت

    Watch Professor El-Shinnawi on your DVD as you read and write this section. This letter has the same shape as the ب , and is also a connector. Instead of one dot underneath, however, it is written with two dots above its body: ت (associate the sound *t* with *two* dots on *top*). In printed text, the two dots are separated, as you see. In handwriting, however, they are often run together into a short horizontal bar (this depends on local practice). (Try to write two dots quickly and you will see how this handwriting form developed.) Practice writing the independent ت by copying the example:

Practice writing ت in initial and medial positions by copying the word تتب (*tatub*) as shown:

Practice writing ت in final position by copying the word بت (*bit*):

DICTATION. WRITE THE WORDS YOU HEAR ON DVD. CLICK ON EACH NUMBER AND LISTEN AS MANY TIMES AS NECESSARY.

1. _____ 3. _____ 5. _____

2. _____ 4. _____ 6. _____

ث

<u>thaa</u>

The fourth letter is pronounced like the first sound in *three*. **Do not** associate this sound with the English letters *th*, because the English spelling represents two quite distinct sounds, each of which has an Arabic equivalent. Pronounce *three* and *that* out loud several times and compare the way you pronounce them. The letter ث represents the sound in *three*, **not** the sound in *that*. Remember this by reminding yourself that this letter has *three* dots, and say *three* out loud before pronouncing or reading ث .

LISTENING EXERCISE 4. *DVD*

LISTEN TO THE DIFFERENCE BETWEEN THE SOUND ث AND THE SOUND *TH* IN *THAT* (ARABIC ذ) UNTIL YOU CAN HEAR IT AND DISTINGUISH ONE FROM THE OTHER. NOTE ALSO THE FRONTAL QUALITY OF BOTH SOUNDS.

جث / جذ   تثوب / تذوب   آثار / آذار   بثور / بذور   ثاب / ذاب

DRILL 3.

DIFFERENTIATE BETWEEN THE SOUNDS IN *THREE* AND *THAT*. SAY THE FOLLOWING WORDS OUT LOUD AND CLASSIFY THEM BELOW ACCORDING TO THE SOUND THEY CONTAIN, <u>TH</u>REE OR <u>TH</u>AT:

they	thumb	teeth	there	throb	thus
although	think	through	brother	together	thought
weather	bother	theft	then	depth	rather

<u>TH</u>REE : _____

<u>TH</u>AT : _____

LISTENING EXERCISE 5. *DVD*

LISTEN TO THE SOUND OF THE LETTER ث ON THE DVD AND REPEAT.

بث   اثاث   تثبت   ثابت   ثاء

ثــ	ـثـ	ـثـ	ث

This letter is a connector, and is written just like ب and ت in all positions, except that it takes *three* dots above. In print, the three dots appear as you see in the box above, but in handwriting, the three dots are usually connected and written as a caret-shaped mark (which can be slightly rounded) as shown in the example below. Watch Professor El-Shinnawi on the DVD and practice writing and saying independent ث :

Copy and practice initial ثـ in the male name ثابت (*thaabit*):

Practice writing medial ـثـ in the word تثبت (*tathbut*):

Write final ـث by copying the word تبث (*tabuth*):

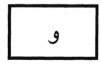
CLICK ON EACH NUMBER, AND CIRCLE THE WORD THAT YOU HEAR:

5. ثابت باثث	3. تاب ثاب	1. باب بات
6. تبت ثبت	4. بث تب	2. بتات ثبات

بـرافـو! (*Bravo!*) You have learned the first four letters of the Arabic alphabet. The next letters in sequence will be presented in Unit Two. Now we will skip ahead to the other two long vowels, and the symbols for the corresponding short vowels.

$$\boxed{\text{و}}$$

uu

This letter represents the second of the three long vowels in Arabic. It is pronounced like the exclamation of delight: *ooooo!* Practice saying this sound and stretch it out, just like you would the exclamation. Remember that the pronunciation of و , like that of alif, should be **twice as long** as normal English vowels.

LISTENING EXERCISE 6.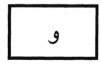

LISTEN TO AND REPEAT THE WORDS CONTAINING و . **GIVE** و **ITS FULL LENGTH IN PRONUNICATION.**

تحبو	تونس	ثبوت	تابوت	توت

WRITING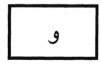

و ـو	و ـو	و	و

Like alif, this letter **does not connect** to any following letter, and therefore its shapes do not vary much. To write independent or initial و , start on the line, loop clockwise to the left and up, then swing down into the tail, which should dip well below the line. Watch the DVD and copy the example:

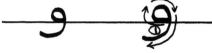

When writing و connected to a previous letter, the joining segment leads into the beginning point of the loop. Copy the example:

و و ‫وـ‬

Now practice writing and pronouncing the word توت *mulberries*:

‫تَوتَ تَوتَ‬

DRILL 5. *DVD*

DICTATION. WRITE THE WORDS YOU HEAR ON DVD.

1. _____   3. _____

2. _____   4. _____

ي

ii

This letter represents the last of the three long vowels, the sound of *ee* in *beep*. Remember that this is a long vowel—hold this sound for **twice as long** as you would hold *ee* in words like *beep, street*, etc.

LISTENING EXERCISE 7. *DVD*

LISTEN TO AND REPEAT THE WORDS CONTAINING ي , GIVING IT FULL LENGTH IN PRONUNCIATION.

تثبتي   ليبي   تثبيت   توبي

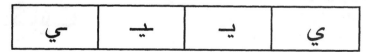

ـي	ـيـ	يـ	ي

As you can see in the box, the independent and final forms of ي differ slightly from the initial and medial forms. Like ب , ت , and ث , which it resembles in its initial and medial shapes, this letter is a connecting one. All shapes of ي retain the two dots below, but, in handwriting, the two dots underneath are usually drawn as a short horizontal bar, just like the dots on top of ت .

To write independent ي , start above the line, and curve slightly upwards and around in an s-like shape. Continue below the line into a wide, flat curve as shown, **making sure to bring the tail all the way back up over the line:**

In final position, start from the connecting segment on the line, then make a small hook into the body. In this position, the letter is almost entirely below the line, and has only a small curved hook before dipping into the wide flat curve. Practice copying and pronouncing ـي **and bring the tail all the way back up over the line:**

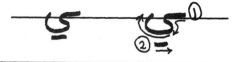

When ي occurs at the beginning or in the middle of a word, it takes the same shape as ت , except that its two dots are below the body of the letter. Copy the example of initial ـيـ :

Now practice writing medial ـيـ in the word تثبيت (*tathbeet*):

تثبيت ①ـيـ ②

DRILL 6. 📀
DICTATION. WRITE THE WORDS YOU HEAR ON THE DVD.

1. _____   3. _____

2. _____   4. _____

i	*u*	*a*

VOWEL LENGTH

Each of the long vowels ا , و , and ي has a short vowel that corresponds to it. The names of these short vowels are fatHa, Damma, and kasra. Each one corresponds in sound to a long vowel: *a* (fatHa) to *aa* (alif), *u* (Damma) to *uu*, and *i* (kasra) to *ii*. The length of the short vowels corresponds to the length of most English vowels, and the length of the long vowels should be at least twice that of a short vowel. (English has no long vowels, so Arabic long vowels should sound and feel extra long to you.) Do not worry about pronouncing a long vowel "too long"—stretch it out so that you can hear the difference. It is important to learn to distinguish between the two lengths in listening and in speaking, because it often corresponds to a difference in meaning.

Short vowels are indicated in Arabic script by markings written above or below the consonant skeleton and dots. Syllables in Arabic always begin with a consonant; by convention, short vowels are written above or below the consonant they follow. Writing vowels is the third and final step in writing a word, after both the skeleton and the dots have been completed. Of course, short vowels are usually not written at all; you have been writing words without them so far.

The following exercises will help you learn to hear and produce the distinction between long and short vowels; repeat them until you can differentiate the two.

LISTENING EXERCISE 8. 🖴

LISTEN TO AND PRONOUNCE THE DIFFERENCES IN VOWEL LENGTH IN THE PAIRS OF WORDS YOU HEAR. THE FIRST WORD IN EACH PAIR CONTAINS A LONG VOWEL AND THE SECOND A SHORT VOWEL. NOTICE THAT VOWEL LENGTH CAN ALSO AFFECT THE WORD STRESS, BECAUSE SYLLABLES WITH LONG VOWELS OFTEN TAKE WORD STRESS.[2]

تقول / تقُل   بير / بِر   شاب / شَب   توب / تُب   ساد / سَد

DRILL 7. 🖴

LISTEN TO THE PAIRS OF WORDS AND REPEAT. CIRCLE THE LETTER CORRESPONDING TO THE WORD THAT CONTAINS A LONG VOWEL.

1.	a	b	3.	a	b	5.	a	b
2.	a	b	4.	a	b	6.	a	b

DRILL 8. 🖴

LISTEN TO THE WORDS ON DVD. MARK L IF YOU HEAR ONE OF THE LONG VOWELS (ا, و, or ي), OR MARK S IF THE WORD HAS ONLY SHORT VOWELS (FATHA, DAMMA, OR KASRA).

1. _____	4. _____	7. _____	10. _____
2. _____	5. _____	8. _____	11. _____
3. _____	6. _____	9. _____	12. _____

a (fatHa)

The short vowel that corresponds to alif is called *fatHa*. Like its long counterpart alif, fatHa ranges in quality from frontal to deep, depending on the quality of the consonants surrounding it. In its most frontal position, fatHa sounds like English *e* as in *bed*. Deep fatHa sounds like English *u* in *but*. Consonants ت, ب, and ث are frontal ones, so they give fatHa a frontal quality, like *e* in *bed*. The name fatHa means *opening*, and refers to the shape of the mouth in pronouncing it: open. Try it and see!

LISTENING EXERCISE 9. 🖴

LISTEN TO AND REPEAT THE WORDS CONTAINING ALIF AND FATHA. PAY SPECIAL ATTENTION TO THE DIFFERENCE IN VOWEL LENGTH.

ثَبات   تابَت   باتَت   تابَ   ثابَت

---

[2]Word stress in Arabic varies somewhat according to regional dialect. In general, formal Arabic word stress falls on the third syllable from the end of the word except if the second-to-last syllable contains a long vowel. Egyptian pronunciation favors the penultimate syllable.

Writing

Arabic words consist of syllables that always begin with consonants, followed by either a short or long vowel. Short vowels are written on top of the letter that precedes them, the first letter of the syllable. FatHa is written as a short slanted line segment above its consonant, as in the word ثَبَتَ . Copy the example:

ثَبَتَ   ثَبَتَ   ـَ ـَ ـَ

_____

_____

Drill 9. 🖸

LISTEN TO THE WORDS ON DVD AND WRITE FATHA WHERE YOU HEAR IT:

1.	تثبيت	3.	بات	5.	ثبت
2.	بتات	4.	ثبات	6.	ثابت

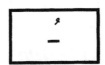

u (Damma)

The short vowel that corresponds to و is called *Damma*, and is pronounced like *oo* as in *booth* when following frontal consonants. When it is affected by deep consonants, it is a little bit deeper, somewhat like *oo* in *wool*.

Do not confuse this vowel with English *o* and *u*, which represent many different sounds, some of them closer to deep fatHa than to Damma. **Remember:** English *u* in words like *but* and *gum* actually represents the sound of a deep fatHa, not a Damma. The name *Damma* refers to the correct shape of the mouth in pronunciation: *rounding*. As long as you keep your mouth rounded, you will pronounce Damma correctly.

Listening Exercise 10. 🖸

LISTEN TO AND REPEAT THE WORDS CONTAINING DAMMA, ROUNDING YOUR MOUTH AS YOU DO SO. LISTEN FOR TWO WORDS THAT CONTAIN BOTH DAMMA AND WAAW AND PRACTICE THE DIFFERENCE IN VOWEL LENGTH.

تَثَبُّت   صُب   حُبوب   ثُبوت   بُث   تُب

WRITING 📀

$$\overset{\text{ُ}}{\underline{}}$$

Damma is written like a miniature و on top of the letter that precedes it, as in the word تُب . Practice writing ◌ُ as shown:

تُب   تُب <u>   </u>

<u> </u>

<u> </u>

$$\overset{}{\underset{\text{ِ}}{\underline{}}}$$

i (kasra)

The short vowel that corresponds to ي is called *kasra*, and its pronunciation ranges from frontal *ee* as in *keep* to deep *i* as in *bit*. As with fatHa and Damma, the exact pronunciation of kasra depends on surrounding consonants. Frontal consonants like ت and ث give kasra a frontal quality. The name kasra *break* refers to the fact that your mouth is slightly *cracked* open in pronouncing it (as opposed to the broad fatHa opening).

LISTENING **E**XERCISE **11.** 📀
LISTEN TO AND REPEAT THE WORDS CONTAINING KASRA.

كِتابي   تُحِب   طِب   بِت   تُثْبِتي   ثِب

WRITING 📀

$$\underset{\text{ِ}}{\underline{}}$$

Kasra is written as a short slanted line segment under the letter it follows, as in ثِب Copy the example:

ثِب   ثِب <u>   </u>

<u> </u>

<u> </u>

Drill 10.

IN THIS SCHOOLBOOK TEXT, FIND FIVE EXAMPLES OF EACH OF THE SHORT VOWELS AND CIRCLE THE LETTERS YOU RECOGNIZE.

كُرَةُ السَّلَّة

نَزَلَ التَّلاميذُ إلى مَلعَبِ المَدرَسَةِ فَرِحينَ ، وَالحَماسَةُ تَملأ نُفوسَهُم. فَدَرسُ الرِّياضَةِ اليَومَ مُباراة في كُرَةِ السَّلَّةِ ، بَينَ فَريق القُمصانِ الحَمراءِ ،وفَريق القُمصانِ الخَضراء .

من «كتاب القراءة للصف الرابع الابتدائي» ، ج. ٢، وزارة التربية السورية، ١٩٨٦

Drill 11. *DVD*

LISTEN TO THESE WORDS ON DVD AND WRITE ALL THE SHORT VOWELS THAT YOU HEAR:

1. ثبتت	3. تبيت	5. تثبت
2. تبت	4. تتوب	6. ثبوت

Drill 12. *DVD*

DICTATION. WRITE THE WORDS YOU HEAR ON DVD.

1. _____   3. _____   5. _____   7. _____

2. _____   4. _____   6. _____   8. _____

Drill 13. *DVD*

READ THE FOLLOWING WORDS ALOUD WITH YOUR DVD:

1. بَث	5. ثَبات	9. توبي
2. بابي	6. تَبات	10. تيتو
3. تُثبِت	7. تابا	11. ثابَت
4. ثُب	8. ثابِت	12. تَثبيت

- 24 -

DRILL 14.

CONNECT THE LETTERS TO FORM WORDS, AS SHOWN IN THE EXAMPLE. SOUND THE WORDS OUT AS YOU WRITE THEM.

EXAMPLE: ــــــــ تــاب ــــــــ = ت + ا + ب

1. ــــــــــــــــــ = ب + ا + ت + ا

2. ــــــــــــــــــ = ثَ + ب + ا + ت + ي

3. ــــــــــــــــــ = ب + ا + ب + ا

4. ــــــــــــــــــ = تَ + بَ + ثَ

5. ــــــــــــــــــ = ي + ا + ب + ب

6. ــــــــــــــــــ = ي + ب + و + ت

7. ــــــــــــــــــ = تَ + ب + تُ

8. ــــــــــــــــــ = ت + و + ب + ا

9. ــــــــــــــــــ = ي + ت + بِ + ث + تُ

10. ــــــــــــــــــ = ت + ب + ي + تَ

11. ــــــــــــــــــ = ي + ت + ي + ب

VOCABULARY DVD
READ AND LEARN THIS WORD:

باب

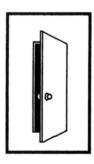

DIALOGUES DVD

    This section on your DVD will introduce you to greetings and frequently used phrases in spoken Arabic. Listen to the scenes with your teacher several times. Try to guess what is going on and what is being said before asking your teacher so that you build guessing techniques, which are crucial to language learning. After you have understood what is being said, go back and listen a few more times to focus on how it is being said. Then you will be ready to imitate the speakers and use the forms as they do to talk about yourself and interact with others.

SCENE ONE: AHLAN WA SAHLAN! GREETINGS AND INTRODUCTIONS

In this unit you will watch Arabs from various countries say hello and introduce themselves. What information do the speakers give? What similarities and differences do you hear? You will hear the speakers in both formal and informal speech registers. What differences do you hear? Choose a speaker and style to imitate and create an introduction you can give in Arabic.

CULTURE: SAYING HELLO 📀

Polite behavior requires you to say hello to everyone in a room or place you enter. The same principle also applies to a loosely defined "space" that someone regularly occupies, such as an outdoor work area, or a guard's position outside a building. Listen to the following most frequently used greetings on your DVD. Learn to recognize and respond to all of them, and choose one to use actively:

Hello or *welcome*; to welcome someone to one's home or workplace; commonly used to say hello in Egypt and North Africa	*ahlan wa sahlan*
reply	*ahlan biik* (male)
	ahlan biiki (female)
Good morning; used everywhere	*SabaaH il-kheer*
reply	*SabaaH in-nuur*
Good evening; used everywhere	*masaa' il-kheer*
reply	*masaa' in-nuur*
Hello; common in Lebanon, Syria, Palestine, Jordan	*marHaba* or *marHaban*
reply	*ahlan* or *marHabtayn*
Greetings; "Islamic" in connotation	*as-salaamu ʿalaykum*
reply	*waʿalaykum us-salaam*

CULTURE: ARABIC DIALECTS 📀

Every language has different registers, that is, the forms of language vary according to speaker and situation. For example, *I dunno* is rarely written, except for special effect, and *I do not know* is rarely used in speech. *Hoagie, submarine, sub, wedge,* and *hero* all refer to the same sandwich, and American southerners often distinguish between singular *you* and plural *y'all*. Americans, Britons, and Australians learn to understand each other's accents merely by being exposed to them.

With its long history and large geographical distribution, Arabic shows some relatively large differences in its written and spoken forms. Names for different registers of Arabic include Modern Standard, Colloquial (often designated by city or country, as in Egyptian Colloquial or Cairene Arabic), and Classical Arabic. In this book, the terms "formal" and "spoken" will be used to differentiate between written and spoken registers of the language.

All varieties of Arabic share the same basic grammar and most vocabulary. Daily life vocabulary shows the largest variation from region to region. Pronunciation (accent) also varies from region to region. For some examples of these differences, listen to a few expressions from four regions: **DVD**

	Cairo	Beirut	Fez	Baghdad
Good morning!	SabaaH il-*kheer*	SabaaH l-*kheer*	SbaH l*khir*	SbaaH l*kheer*
How are you? (masculine)	izzayyak?	kiifak?	laa baas?	shloonak?
Good, fine	kuwayyis	mniiH	mzyan	zein
Goodbye	ma^{c}a ssalaama	ma^{c}a ssalaame	bsslama	ma^{c}a ssalaama

As you can see and hear, the accents are different and some of the expressions vary, although they are all related to formal Arabic. Notice, for example, the consistent use of *ak* or *k* for *your*. The more formal Arabic you know, the easier it is to recognize the dialect forms that are related to it.

In this textbook series, you will focus on learning to read and write modern formal Arabic. You will also learn to speak in simplified formal Arabic while being introduced to common expressions used in daily life in Egypt through the DVD. The Egyptian dialect is widely understood throughout the Arab world, thanks to the popularity of Egyptian films, songs, and television shows.

To be fluent in Arabic, you must have control of both the formal and spoken registers. It is quite natural to mix the two, and this is a skill that native speakers develop over the course of their formal and social education. You will develop this skill too; after all, you already shift from one level to another naturally in your native language. The more Arabic you learn, the easier it will become to recognize, understand, and use the different registers of Arabic.

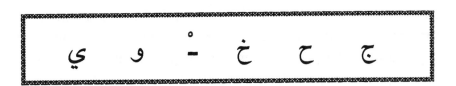

الوحدة الثانية
UNIT TWO

ي	و	- ْ	خ	ح	ج

In this unit you will learn three more consonants, more about the letters و and ي , and the symbol that indicates the absence of a short vowel. Two of the three consonant sounds introduced in this unit have no English equivalent. Learn to pronounce them properly now, and practice to develop the muscles you use to pronounce these sounds. Spend five or ten minutes, three times a day, practicing these sounds with the DVD.

The three new consonants represent the next three letters in the alphabet after ث . Just as ب , ت , and ث share the same skeletal shape and are distinguished by the number and position of the dots, so these three letters have the same basic shapes, but are distinguished by their dots.

ج

jiim (giim)

The letter *jiim* has three different pronunciations that vary according to region in the Arab world. In the Arabian Peninsula and surrounding areas, it is pronounced like *j* in *jack* or *dg* in *bridge*. In much of the Levant and North Africa, it is pronounced like the French *j* in *bonjour* (a sound often represented in English by *s* as in *pleasure* or *decision*). In Cairo, it is pronounced like the hard *g* in *game*.

LISTENING EXERCISE 1. DVD
LISTEN TO THE WORDS AS THEY ARE PRONOUNCED IN THE THREE DIALECT VARIATIONS.

دَجاج	تُجيب	جُب	تاج

Learn to recognize all three pronunciations of ج and choose one to use when speaking.

WRITING DVD

جّ	ج	ج	ج

This chart shows you that the shapes of ج and its sister letters vary a little from one position to the other in print. In handwriting, these letters are connected in a different way

- 28 -

than the print version shown here. It will be helpful to watch Professor El-Shinnawi write the shapes of ح and similar letters on your DVD as you learn to write these letters.

As the initial and medial shapes of this letter suggest, ح is a connector. To write ح alone, start at a point well above the line, make a small hook, then draw a line straight across, then change direction and swing down well below the line into the tail. Follow the arrows and imitate the shape that you see:

To write ــج in initial position, begin with the hook as you did above, then slant down toward the line into a point just above the line, and then, instead of curving down into the tail, continue into the connecting segment as shown:

Practice writing the word جاب (*he brought*):

When this letter is connected on both sides, it takes the following shape in printed text: ـجـ as in تُجِيب . **However, it is not written this way by hand.** To write this letter in the middle of a word, you must plan ahead, because the connecting segment lies well above the line, at the highest point of this letter. This means that you need to end the previous letter above the line. In the following example, the combination ـتجـ is written by starting and drawing the ـت completely above the line dropping down into the ـجـ . Note the difference between the shape of the ـت as Professor El-Shinnawi writes it on the DVD and as it is

written here; both forms are common. Copy the word تُجيب as it is written:

In word-final position, ج takes the same tail it has independently. There are two ways to reach the starting point of a medial or final ج . In the first, a connecting segment is drawn from the line up and then over as the example shows. Watch Professor El-Shinnawi on your DVD and copy the word بيج (*beige*) as it is written this way:

In the second, the preceding letter or letters are written above the line so that the connecting segment can flow into ج at the same level as the example shows. Copy the word بيج as it is written the second way here:

Copy these words to practice writing medial and final ج with connecting segments:

تُجاب بُجاب تَبُج تَبُج تَبُج

DICTATION. WRITE THE WORDS YOU HEAR.

1. _____   3. _____   5. _____

2. _____   4. _____   6. _____

ح

Haa

The letter *Haa* represents a sound that is pronounced deep in the throat. It has no equivalent in English. First, take a few minutes to become better acquainted with some of your throat muscles that you use often, but not to speak English. The following exercises are designed to make you aware of what these muscles can already do, so that you can use them to speak Arabic. Practice them for a few minutes every day, as often as you can.

Exercise 1. With your mouth closed, block off your windpipe at your throat. Put your hand on your throat at the Adam's apple and constrict the muscles on the inside. You should be able to feel the muscles contracting. Alternately tighten and relax them for a few minutes.

Exercise 2. Repeat this with your mouth open. Try to breathe out through your mouth—if you can, you are not closing off the windpipe entirely.

Exercise 3. Constrict those same muscles so that air can just barely squeeze through your throat. Imitate someone fogging a pair of glasses to clean them. By now, you should be aware of what your throat muscles are doing.

Exercise 4. Bend your head down so that your chin rests on the top of your chest, and repeat Exercise 3. This position should make it easier for you to feel what you are doing.

Pronouncing ح takes practice, first to pronounce the letter alone, and then to pronounce it surrounded by other letters in a word. You must learn to pronounce it properly to be understood, and at first, this will take some concentration on your part. The more you practice now, the sooner you will be able to say it easily.

LISTENING EXERCISE 2. DVD

LISTEN TO THE SOUND OF ح **IN VARIOUS POSITIONS AND REPEAT. DO THIS AS MANY TIMES AS YOU CAN AND REPEAT THIS DRILL DAILY UNTIL YOU CAN PRONOUNCE THIS SOUND EASILY.**

صَباح   تَبوح   بَحث   حَبيب

ح	ح	ح	ح

Like ج , ح is a connector. It is written exactly like ج , except that it has no dot. Practice writing initial ح in the word حَبيب (*darling*):

_____

_____

Now practice writing and pronouncing medial ـحـ in تَحت (*below*). Remember to plan ahead and write the preceding letter above the line so that you can begin ـحـ from above. Copy:

_____

_____

Sometimes two of these letters occur together in juxtaposition. Here too you must give yourself room to connect into the second letter by writing the first one well above the line. Do **not** pick your pen up and break the skeletal structure of the word. Copy the example and practice writing حِجاب (*veil, hijab*):

_____

_____

Final ـح is written with the tail. Copy the word تُبيح :

_____

_____

- 32 -

DRILL 2. DVD

DICTATION. WRITE THE WORDS YOU HEAR ON THE DVD.

1. _____   3. _____   5. _____

2. _____   4. _____   6. _____

$$\boxed{\;\; \text{خ} \;\;}$$

khaa

The sound of the letter *khaa* is found in many European languages: the Russian *x*, the Scottish pronunciation of *loch*, and German *ch* as pronounced after a back vowel as in *Bach*. Some people use this sound to say *yech!* To pronounce خ, say *k* and pay attention to where the back of your tongue hits the back of the roof of your mouth and blocks your windpipe. Instead of closing off the windpipe with the back of your tongue completely, block it part way, and you will produce this sound.

LISTENING EXERCISE 3. DVD

LISTEN TO AND REPEAT THESE WORDS CONTAINING خ ON THE DVD.

تَختي   بَخت   باخ   بَخيل   خاب

WRITING DVD

ـخ	ـخـ	خـ	خ

Like its sisters, خ is a connector, and its shapes are written exactly as the ones you learned for ج and ح , except that it takes one dot above. Practice writing initial خ in the word خاب , saying it as you write:

خاب

_____

_____

Practice writing and pronouncing medial خ in بخت (*luck*):

Now practice final خ by copying the word بَخ :

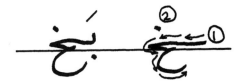

DRILL 3. *DVD*

YOU WILL HEAR TWELVE WORDS, EACH CONTAINING ج ، ح ، OR خ; WRITE THE LETTER YOU HEAR IN EACH WORD:

1. _____   4. _____   7. _____   10. _____

2. _____   5. _____   8. _____   11. _____

3. _____   6. _____   9. _____   12. _____

DRILL 4. *DVD*

CONNECT THE FOLLOWING LETTERS TO FORM WORDS, THEN LISTEN TO THE WORDS ON **DVD** AND MARK IN THE SHORT VOWELS WHERE YOU HEAR THEM:

1. _____ = خ + ا + ب + ت   5. _____ = ت + ج + و + ب

2. _____ = ح + ج + ا + ب   6. _____ = ب + ث + و + ح

3. _____ = ح + ب + ي + ب   7. _____ = ت + ب + و + ح + ي

4. _____ = ت + خ + و + ت   8. _____ = ح + ج + ب + ت

DRILL 5. *DVD*
DICTATION.

1. _____   3. _____   5. _____

2. _____   4. _____   6. _____

DVD

READ THESE WORDS ALOUD, PAYING SPECIAL ATTENTION TO VOWEL LENGTH AND THE SOUNDS ح AND خ .

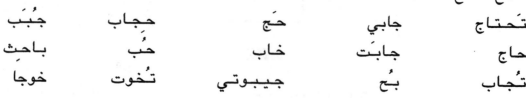

جُبَب	حِجاب	حَج	جابي	تَحتاج
باحِث	حُب	خاب	جابَت	حاج
خوجا	تُخوت	جيبوتي	بُح	تُجاب

○
ー

sukuun

This symbol is a pronunciation marker that indicates the absence of a short vowel. So far, you have learned to use fatHa, Damma, and kasra over consonants to indicate the short vowels, and consonants not followed by a vowel have been left "blank." In fully vowelled texts, however, all consonants have at least one marking, even if no vowel occurs, because there is a special symbol to indicate the absence of a vowel. This symbol is called *sukuun* (meaning *silence*).

To see how sukuun works, listen to and study the words below in Arabic script and in transliteration broken down syllable by syllable. Note that every syllable that ends in a consonant takes a sukuun, indicating that there is no vowel and hence no new syllable.

بَحْثي	تُثْبِتي	تَحْجُبُ	تَخْتي	تَحْتَج
baH - thii	tuth - bí - tii	taH - ju - bu	takh - tii	taH - taj

LISTENING EXERCISE 4. **DVD**

LISTEN TO THE WORDS YOU STUDIED ABOVE AND PRACTICE READING THEM BY SYLLABLE.

WRITING

○
ー

Like the short vowel symbols, the sukuun is rarely used in unvowelled or partially vowelled texts. When it is written, it appears as a small open circle above a letter not followed by a vowel. In writing sukuun, make sure to draw a closed circle and not a Damma or a dot. Copy the examples:

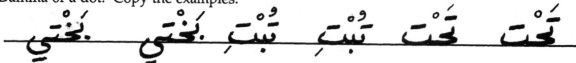

و

waaw

In Unit One, you learned that و represents the long vowel sound "uu." It also has a second function, related to the first one: when preceded or followed by a long or short vowel, this letter is pronounced *w* as in *well*, or as in the name of the letter: واو "waaw." To see how these two sounds are related, pronounce *oo* and hold it *ooooooooooo* then go right into *a*. You will hear a *w* sound connecting the two vowels. At the beginning of a word, و will always be pronounced *w*, because Arabic words cannot begin with a vowel. **Remember:** any vowel, short or long, preceding or following و turns it into a consonant.

LISTENING EXERCISE 5. 🆅

LISTEN TO AND REPEAT THE WORDS CONTAINING CONSONANT و .

خَاوِي   حِوَار   جَوَاب   وَاجِب   وَثَبَ

Just as *w* occurs in diphthongs[1] in English, so does و in Arabic. However, Arabic has only one diphthong with و , which is ـَوْ (و preceded by a fatHa). The sound of this combination is similar to the *ow* sound in *crown* or *town*. (Do not confuse pronunciation and spelling; there are several different diphthong sounds in English and their spellings overlap.)

In unvowelled texts, this diphthong is usually not indicated; however, it may be indicated by a fatHa on the preceding letter **or a sukuun on** و **or both.** The following are three different ways of vocalizing the word خوخ (*peach*):

خَوخ   =   خَوْخ   =   خَوْخ

The sukuun alone can indicate this sound because it can only occur on consonants, so if you see ـوْ , you know that the letter is functioning as a consonant, and that a vowel precedes it. In such a case, the vowel must be a fatHa .

LISTENING EXERCISE 6. 🆅

LISTEN TO THE SOUND OF THE DIPHTHONG ـَوْ AND REPEAT.

حَوْل   خَوْخ   تَوبِيخ   زَوج   ثَوب

---

[1]A diphthong is a combination of vowel and semi-vowel sounds, such as *ow* in *cow*, *ow* in *mow*, or *a w* in *saw*.

DRILL 7. 📀
DICTATION.

1. _____   3. _____

2. _____   4. _____

$$\boxed{\text{ي}}$$

yaa

The long vowel ي also functions as a consonant at the beginning of a word, or when preceded or followed by a vowel: it is pronounced like *y* in *yes*. Say *eeeeeee* and go right into *a* and you will hear yourself say *y*.

LISTENING EXERCISE 7. 📀
LISTEN TO WORDS CONTAINING THE CONSONANT ي AND REPEAT.

يَثـوب   يَجِب   جُيـوب   ثِيـاب   بُيـوت

When ي is preceded by a fatHa and followed by sukuun, it forms a diphthong that is pronounced like *ay* as in *say* (or, if following emphatic letters, like *i* in *like*). The sukuun alone may be written on ي to indicate this diphthong, or the fatHa may be used, or both sukuun and fatHa. Thus there are three different ways of vocalizing the word بيت (*house*):

بَيْت   =   بيت   =   بَيْت

The sukuun alone can indicate these diphthongs because it can only occur on consonants, so if you see ـيْ , you know that the letter is functioning as a consonant and that a vowel precedes it. In this case, the vowel must be a fatHa .

LISTENING EXERCISE 8. 📀
LISTEN TO THE SOUND OF THE DIPHTHONG ـيْ AND REPEAT.

بَيْن   بَيْت   جَيْب   خَيْر   حَيْث

DRILL 8. 📀
DICTATION.

1. _____   3. _____

2. _____   4. _____

DRILL 9. 📀
READ THESE WORDS ALOUD (ACROSS FROM RIGHT TO LEFT):

حَبِيبَتي	حَبِيبي	واجِبات	ثِيابي	يَخْت
تَبوحي	جُيوب	جَيْبي	ثَواب	حَيْث
تُجِيبي	وُجوب	بُيوت	بَيتي	بَحْث
جَوابات	جَواب	جُثَث	يَجِب	خابَ

DRILL 10. 📀
CONNECT THE FOLLOWING LETTERS TO FORM WORDS. THEN LISTEN TO THE WORDS ON DVD AND WRITE IN ALL THE SHORT VOWELS THAT YOU HEAR.

1. _____ = ج + ا + ب + ت
2. _____ = ح + ج + ب
3. _____ = خ + و + خ
4. _____ = ث + ي + ا + ب + ي
5. _____ = ج + ي + ب + و + ت + ي
6. _____ = ح + ب + ي + ب + ت + ي
7. _____ = ب + ح + و + ث
8. _____ = و + ا + ج + ب + ا + ت
9. _____ = ب + ي + و + ت
10. _____ = ج + ي + و + ب

DRILL 11. 📀
DICTATION.

1. _____   3. _____   5. _____

2. _____   4. _____   6. _____

PEUGEOT | بيجو

VOCABULARY 📀
GO TO THE VOCABULARY SECTION ON YOUR DVD AND CLICK ON THESE WORDS TO LISTEN AND LEARN THEM.

حَبيبَتي   حَبيبي   واجِب   بَيْت

DRILL 12.
MATCH THE WORDS YOU LEARNED WITH THE PICTURES BELOW AND WRITE THEM IN ARABIC:

DIALOGUES 📀
SCENE TWO: HADRITIK MIN MASR?

In Unit One, you watched speakers from different countries introduce themselves. Starting here, in Unit Two, the dialogues you watch will be in Egyptian (or , more specifically, Cairene) Arabic. These scenes were filmed in Cairo and are meant to provide an introduction to basic aspects of Arab culture. We have chosen the Cairene dialect because it is the most widely understood dialect in the Arab world, and because almost one in every three Arabic speakers is Egyptian. Your teacher or friends can teach you the dialect forms they use in addition or as an alternative. Dialects can sound quite different at first, and some of the words you will learn from the Egyptian dialogues will vary a bit in other dialects, but the more Arabic you learn, the more overlap you will find. Dialects that are geographically close tend to be linguistically similar.

Watch the scenes with your teacher, who will guide you in understanding and learning the expressions. Watch each dialogue as many times as necessary, at first to understand what is being said, and then to concentrate on exactly **how** it is being said. Remember that you learned your native language by listening and imitating. By learning these expressions through an audiovisual medium, you are utilizing the same skills you used to learn your native language, and you are building listening comprehension skills in Arabic.

CULTURE: HADRITAK / HADRITIK

In Arab culture, politeness is signaled in part by language usage. In Egypt, when meeting someone for the first time, or addressing someone senior to you in age or position, or someone you do not know well, it is impolite to address him or her as "you." Address men with the word *HaDritak* (literally *your presence*), and women with *HaDritik*, to show respect.

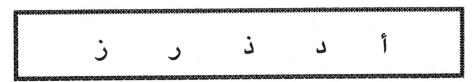

الوحدة الثالثة
UNIT THREE

أ   د   ذ   ر   ز

In this unit you will learn about the second function of alif and the next four consonants in the alphabet. All these consonants are nonconnectors: they do not connect to any following letter.

أ

hamza

In Unit Two you saw that و and ي sometimes function as consonants. Remember that they always function as consonants at the beginning of a word. The letter ا can also represent a consonant sound when it occurs at the beginning of a word. The consonant that it stands for is called *hamza*; you can see its shape on top of the alif in the box above. Hamza is often written on alif, but may also occur alone as ء .

Hamza is not a vowel but rather (like other consonants) is a carrier of vowel sounds. It is a sound you make in English all the time—every time you say a word that begins with a vowel, in fact—but you do not recognize it as a consonant because English has no letter for it.[1] Say *uh-oh* several times and pay attention to the sound you make in between the two syllables. You make the same sound when you pronounce any word that begins with a vowel, such as *our, if, it, I, on, up*. Say these out loud, and pay attention to the "catch" in your throat as you pronounce the first vowel. This sound is not written in English, which treats these words as if they began with a vowel. In Arabic, however, this sound is considered to be a consonant. **Remember:** in Arabic, no word or syllable begins with a vowel. What sounds to English speakers like an Arabic word that begins with a vowel is actually a word that begins with hamza.

When a word begins with hamza, it is always written on an alif "seat" (*kursii*). In everyday print and writing, initial hamza is often, but not always, written on top of the alif that "holds" or represents it. Thus, initial hamza may appear as ا or as أ . **Remember:** alif at the beginning of a word is always a seat for hamza, never a long vowel.

---

[1]In linguistic terminology, this sound is called "glottal stop."

Hamza occurs not only at the beginning, but also in the middle or at the end of a word. (We will introduce the orthography of medial hamza in Unit 9.) For now you will learn to write initial and independent hamza.

LISTENING EXERCISE 1. *DVD*
PRACTICE SAYING HAMZA BY LISTENING TO AND REPEATING THE WORDS ON THE DVD.

أَخَوات   أَب   سَبَأَ   تَأَتَأَ   بَأْس

Hamza has no place of its own in the alphabet, for historical reasons that involve Quranic spelling. Tradition holds that the dialect of Mecca which the Prophet Muhammed spoke did not have this sound, and therefore it was not written when the Quran was first recorded in script. The symbol for the hamza was developed, along with the short vowel markings, at a later date. This is why hamza has several different "spellings," depending on its position in the word and the vowel sounds surrounding it. In this unit you will learn two common spellings, أ and ء .

LISTENING EXERCISE 2. *DVD*
LISTEN TO INITIAL HAMZA IN THE WORDS ON DVD AND REPEAT.

أَثاث   أَخَوات   أَخ   أَتَت   أَب

At the beginning of a word hamza is represented by alif, either ا or أ. However, the vowel sound this alif-hamza represents may be any of the short vowels: fatHa, Damma, or kasra. The words in Listening Exercise 2 all begin with hamza followed by the vowel fatHa. In other cases, the other short vowels may appear in this position; that is, أ serves as a seat for Damma and kasra as well as fatHa. Note that when the initial vowel is kasra, the hamza is often written **underneath** the alif, as in: إِثْبـات . **Remember:** while ا and أ **can** carry the kasra, إ **always** indicates a kasra vowel.

LISTENING EXERCISE 3. *DVD*
LISTEN TO INITIAL HAMZA WITH VOWELS DAMMA AND KASRA AND REPEAT.

إِبْحـار   أُخْت   إِثْبـات   أُخْرِجَ   إِخْبـار   أُثْبِتَ

In fully vocalized texts, the short vowel will be marked. In unvocalized texts, you will see only the consonant skeleton. To read an unvocalized word correctly, you need to know it, or make an educated guess based on knowledge of Arabic word patterns (this will become clear later on). Learn to associate the pronunciation of each new vocabulary item with its consonant frame, the same way you associate certain pronunciations in English with certain spellings (think of *neighbor* and *weigh, taught* and *caught*). In your native language, you read by word, not by syllable, and it is important to develop this same skill in Arabic.

أ	ء

The actual shape of the hamza, shown in the left box above, is a small "c" shape that continues into a line on the bottom. At the beginning of a word, it is always written on alif, and the alif alone may represent it. When it occurs in the middle of a word, it may be written on a seat that has the shape of any of the long vowels: أ , ؤ , or ئ (you will learn more about these spellings of hamza later). When hamza occurs after a long vowel at the end of a word, it is usually written on the line, without a seat, in which case it is a bit larger in size. Copy and practice the shape of independent hamza:

ء   ء①

_____

_____

LISTENING EXERCISE 4. *DVD*

THE NAMES OF MANY LETTERS OF THE ALPHABET END IN HAMZA. LISTEN TO AND REPEAT THE NAMES OF LETTERS YOU HAVE LEARNED.

خاء   حاء   ثاء   تاء   باء

Practice writing and pronouncing final hamza by copying the names of these letters:

خاء خاء حاء حاء ثاء ثاء تاء تاء باء باء

_____

_____

Practice writing initial hamza on alif by copying أخ (brother), أخت (sister), and إثبات (proof):

إثبات إثبات أخت أخت أخ أخ

_____

_____

DRILL 1. 📀

YOU WILL HEAR TWELVE WORDS. WRITE ٴ FOR EACH WORD IN WHICH YOU HEAR IT:

1. _____   4. _____   7. _____   10. _____

2. _____   5. _____   8. _____   11. _____

3. _____   6. _____   9. _____   12. _____

DRILL 2. 📀
DICTATION.

1. _____   3. _____   5. _____

2. _____   4. _____   6. _____

د

daal

This consonant is pronounced like a clear, frontal *d* in English, as in the word *dentist* (**not** like the *d* sound in *puddle*). Pay particular attention to your pronunciation of medial and final د , and to the surrounding vowel sounds, which should be frontal in quality (remember *a* in *bad* and *e* in *bet*).

LISTENING EXERCISE 5. 📀

LISTEN TO AND READ ALOUD THE WORDS CONTAINING د .

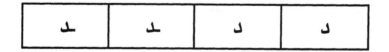

أَحْداث   أَدَب   جَديد   حُدود   خُدود   دَجاج

WRITING 📀

ـد	ـد	د	د

The letter د does not connect to any letter that follows it. To write initial د , begin well above the line, and slant down as shown below. Just before hitting the line, angle sharply and finish along the line into a tiny hook. In handwriting, the exact shape and slant of this letter vary slightly according to individual style, but it is important to keep the angle of the body of this letter **less** than 90 degrees and to keep it **above** the line. Watch Professor El-Shinnawi on your DVD and copy the examples:

To write د when it is connected to a previous letter in medial or final position, begin from the connecting segment, draw the top half of the letter from the line up, then trace your line back down, make a sharp angle as before, and finish. When connected from the previous letter, the top half of the angle tends to have a slightly different shape because of the connecting segment. Copy:

Now practice by copying the words دَجاج (chicken) and جَديد (new):

جَديد جَديد دَجاج دَجاج جَديد جَديد دَجاج دَجاج

ذ

dhaal

In Unit One, you learned to distinguish between the sound *th* in *three*, represented in Arabic by the letter ث , and the sound *th* in the word *other*. The letter ذ represents the *other* sound (pun intended—remember it this way!).

LISTENING EXERCISE 6. DVD
LISTEN TO WORDS CONTAINING ذ AND READ ALOUD.

تَذبْذُب   حَذارِ   خُذْ   بَذَرَ   ذات   ذُباب

WRITING 📀

ﻧ	ﻨ	ذ	ذ

The letter ذ is written just like ر , except that it takes a single dot above. Like ر , it does not connect to a following letter, and so has only two forms, initial/independent and medial/final. Practice the initial/independent form by copying ذُبـاب (*flies*):

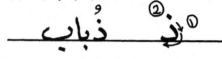

Practice writing the medial/final form by copying خُذ (*take!*):

Now copy and read aloud these words:

أَخَـذْتُ (*I took*)   يَذوب (*it melts*)   ذات (*self*)

DRILL 3. 📀

YOU WILL HEAR TWELVE WORDS ON DVD, EACH CONTAINING EITHER ذ OR ث . CIRCLE THE SOUND YOU HEAR IN EACH WORD.

1.	ث	ذ	5.	ث	ذ	9.	ث	ذ
2.	ث	ذ	6.	ث	ذ	10.	ث	ذ
3.	ث	ذ	7.	ث	ذ	11.	ث	ذ
4.	ث	ذ	8.	ث	ذ	12.	ث	ذ

Drill 4. ⊙

Read the following words aloud with the DVD, paying particular attention to the pronunciation of ث and ذ .

1. ذابَ	3. ذُباب	5. ثَواب	7. جُثَث
2. ثابَ	4. ثَبات	6. ذَوات	8. جاذِب

Drill 5. ⊙

You will hear eight words. For each, write the missing letter in the blank:

1. تَ ___ وب	3. ___ ات	5. ___ وبي	7. أ ___ ا
2. ___ خُوَ	4. أ ___ واب	6. جَ ___ ب	8. خُ ___ ي

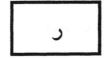

raa

This is the name of the Arabic *r*. It is a flap, like the Spanish or Italian *r*. You already know how to make this sound: it is the sound American English speakers make saying *gotta* as in *gotta go*. Say *gotta* several times in a row very quickly and pay attention to what your tongue is doing. You should feel it flapping against the roof of your mouth behind your teeth. Now pronounce the sound alone. Another good exercise is to practice making a whirring sound: *rrrrrrrrrrr*. Do these exercises daily until you have mastered this sound, and go back to the alphabet chart in the Introduction to watch it being pronounced.

Listening Exercise 7. ⊙

Listen to and read aloud words containing ر . Note that ر often deepens the quality of alif and fatHa so that they sound like *a* in *father* .

وُرود	جار	تَبْرير	خَراج	رُدود	رَباب

Writing ⊙

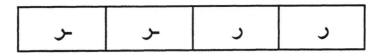

This letter is a nonconnector, and is written almost entirely below the line. You will see that the exact angle and shape of the ر vary somewhat in handwriting and print styles, but it may be distinguished from و by its wide angle and its long tail that dips well below

the line (remember that ‎د‎ rests on the line). To write initial ‎ر‎ , begin on the line and curve downwards below it. Imitate the shape in the example:

To write ‎ـر‎ connected from a previous letter, start from the connecting segment on the line, then curve down. You can see a slight "tooth" at the beginnning of this letter in print fonts, but this is omitted in handwriting. Copy:

‎ز‎

zaay

This consonant corresponds to the English sound *z* in *zebra*.

LISTENING EXERCISE 8. DVD

LISTEN TO AND READ ALOUD WORDS CONTAINING THE SOUND ‎ز‎ ON THE DVD.

تَزيـد   جَواز   يَزور   زُجاج   أحْزاب   زَوْج

WRITING DVD

ـز	ـز	ز	ز

The letter ‎ز‎ is a nonconnector, and has the same shape as ‎ر‎ , except that it takes one dot above. Practice writing initial/independent ‎ز‎ by copying the word ‎زَوْج‎ (*husband*):

Copy ـز in medial/final position in the word خُبز (bread):

_____

_____

DRILL 6 📀

DICTATION. LISTEN TO THE FEMALE AND MALE NAMES ON DVD AND WRITE THEM OUT. NAMES 1-5 ARE FEMALE, 6-10 ARE MALE.

1. _____   6. _____

2. _____   7. _____

3. _____   8. _____

4. _____   9. _____

5. _____   10. _____

DRILL 7. 📀

CONNECT THE LETTERS TO FORM WORDS, THEN LISTEN TO THEM ON DVD AND WRITE IN THE SHORT VOWELS:

1. _____ = ذ + ا + ذ + ر   8. _____ = د + و + د + ح

2. _____ = ر + د + ا + خ   9. _____ = د + و + د + ر

3. _____ = د + ر + ز   10. _____ = ر + ي + ذ + ح + ت

4. _____ = ب + و + ر + ح   11. _____ = ر + ا + و + د + أ

5. _____ = ر + ا + ج + ء   12. _____ = ج + ر + خ + ي

6. _____ = ر + ا + ح + ب   13. _____ = ب + ا + ر + ج + ت

7. _____ = ج + ا + و + ز + أ   14. _____ = ت + ح + ب + ذ

محوح Dodge محوح

- 48 -

1. _____   6. _____

2. _____   7. _____

3. _____   8. _____

4. _____   9. _____

5. _____   10. _____

DRILL 9.
READ THE FOLLOWING WORDS ALOUD:

دار	واحِد	حِزْب	وَرْد
زُيـوت	أزرار	بَيْـروت	إخْبار
زُجاج	أبي	يَجري	تَأْثير
تَثاءَبَ	خَرَز	ذَوات	تَحْذير
دَجاج	بازار	بير زَيْت	بارِد
أخْت	حُروب	زَيْت	وَحيد
جَرير	أحْزاب	أخَوات	ثَأر
وُزَراء	ثَوْر	يَدور	بَحْري

DIALOGUE *DVD*
WATCH SCENE 3 IZZAYY HADRITIK? AND SCENE 4 SABAAH IL-KHEER!

CULTURE: MEETING AND GREETING PEOPLE

In Arab culture, it is considered rude not to say good morning, good evening, or hello to people you know, even casually, the first time you see them each day. In addition, when you enter a room or any kind of defined or enclosed space, you should greet people who are already there, whether you know them or not.

In social situations, it is polite to shake hands upon meeting or greeting another person, especially someone of the same gender. Some people do not shake hands with members of the opposite sex; this is a matter of personal preference or religious belief. Close friends of the same gender often greet each other by kissing on both cheeks.

AL-HAMDU LILLAAH

Literally *Praise be to God, Thank God*, this is one of the most widely used phrases in Arabic by people of all religious backgrounds. Its most common uses are (a) in response to *How are you?* whether or not one is well, because God is to be thanked at all times, (b) upon finishing a meal, to signal that one has had enough, and (c) upon successfully completing a task or learning of a positive outcome.

VOCABULARY

LISTEN TO AND LEARN THESE WORDS ON DVD (MEANINGS INCLUDE *SISTER, BROTHER, ONE, CHICKEN, NEWS, BREAD, AND NEIGHBOR*):

جار   دَجاج   خُبز   أخبار

جَديد *NEW*   واحِد   أُخت   أخ

DRILL 10.

MATCH THE WORDS YOU LEARNED WITH THESE PICTURES:

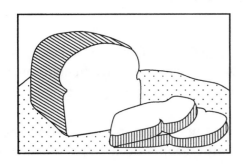

الوحدة الرابعة
UNIT FOUR

ضَ ص ش س ـّ

In this unit you will learn the symbol for doubling consonants and the next four letters of the alphabet in sequence.

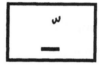

shadda

      This symbol, called *shadda*, is a pronunciation marker whose function is to double **the length of a consonant in pronunciation. Do not** associate the shadda with two identical, **consecutive consonants in English, as in the word** *little*; in English, doubling is merely a **spelling convention that may affect the vowel sound, but not the pronunciation of the consonant itself.** In Arabic, doubling **changes the pronunciation** of the consonant over which it is written and **affects the meaning** of any word in which it occurs. Like other vocalization marks, shadda is usually omitted in unvowelled texts, except where ambiguity **might arise without it.** In general, the reader is expected to know which words take shadda, **and to use context, if necessary, to guess.**

      Any consonant may be doubled as long as it does not begin a word. The difference between a single consonant and a doubled one is one of length: a doubled consonant is pronounced and held for **twice as long** as a single one. This is easy to do with fluid sounds, like ث, ذ, ر, خ, ح, ج, ر, and ز. To double the sounds ب, ت, and د, you must begin to say them and pause in the middle of pronouncing them for a second. Practice this by doing the following exercise.

LISTENING EXERCISE 1. **DVD**
CONTRAST CONSONANTS WITH AND WITHOUT SHADDA BY LISTENING TO AND REPEATING THE PAIRS OF WORDS ON DVD. IN EACH CASE, THE SHADDA MAKES A DIFFERENCE IN MEANING.

خَرَجَ / خَرَّجَ   شاب / شابّ   حاجة / حاجّة   دَرَسَ / دَرَّسَ   تَجِدُ / تَجِدُّ

Drill 1. 📀

You will hear twelve words. Mark X if you hear a shadda:

1. _____   4. _____   7. _____   10. _____

2. _____   5. _____   8. _____   11. _____

3. _____   6. _____   9. _____   12. _____

Writing 📀

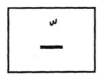

Shadda is written like a tiny, rounded w on top of the consonant that it doubles. Practice by copying the word حَجّ (*pilgrimage*):

حَجّ حَجّ

_____

_____

Practice writing and reading shadda in these words:

(*I love*) أُحِبّ   (*baker*) خَبّاز   (*he marries*) يَتَزَوّج

_____

_____

Shadda and the Short Vowels

A consonant that has a shadda must have a vowel as well, because formal Arabic does not allow more than two consonants to occur together without a vowel.[1] When writing the vowels on shadda, remember that fatHa and Damma are always written **above** the shadda. When writing shadda + kasra, you have two options: (a) the kasra may be written in its normal position beneath the line, such that the shadda sits above and the kasra below the consonant: ﹼ or (b) the kasra may be written just below the shadda above the consonant: ﹼ. Learn to recognize both forms and choose one to use. Copy the examples:

---

[1]This rule holds as well for shadda at the end of a word, but the vowel in this case is often a grammatical ending. We will introduce these grammatical endings in Unit 10.

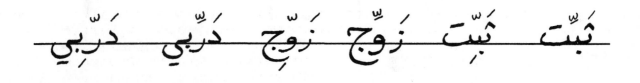

DISTINGUISHING BETWEEN DOUBLED CONSONANTS AND LONG VOWELS

Distinguishing between a consonant doubled with a shadda and a long vowel sound requires practice and repetition. Practice the drills below repeatedly over the next couple of weeks until you feel confident in your comprehension and production of this difference.

LISTENING EXERCISE 2. DVD

COMPARE THE PAIRS OF WORDS ON THE DVD, THE FIRST OF WHICH HAS A LONG VOWEL AND THE SECOND A SHADDA. LISTEN AND REPEAT ALOUD UNTIL YOU CAN HEAR THE DIFFERENCE.

دوري/دُرّي   دارِس/دَرِّس   تَزاوَجَ /تَزَوَّجَ   جاوَزَ /جَوَّزَ   راجَعَ / رَجَّعَ

DRILL 2. DVD

YOU WILL HEAR TWELVE WORDS, EACH CONTAINING EITHER A SHADDA OR A LONG VOWEL. SOME WORDS CONTAIN و AND ي AS CONSONANTS, IN WHICH CASE THEY CAN TAKE SHADDA (YOU HEARD EXAMPLES OF THIS IN LISTENING EXERCISE 2). INDICATE WHICH WORDS CONTAIN LONG VOWELS AND WHICH SHADDA BY WRITING EITHER THE LONG VOWEL YOU HEAR OR SHADDA:

1. _____   4. _____   7. _____   10. _____

2. _____   5. _____   8. _____   11. _____

3. _____   6. _____   9. _____   12. _____

DRILL 3. DVD
DICTATION.

1. _____   4. _____

2. _____   5. _____

3. _____   6. _____

س

siin

Siin (pronounced "seen") is the name of the Arabic letter corresponding to English s as in the word *seen* itself. However, remember that English s represents several different sounds, the most common of which is z (a sound it often takes in between vowels, such as in *easy*, or as a plural ending, as in *dogs* or *bugs*). Arabic س , on the other hand, always retains the soft *sssss* sound. س is a frontal consonant, which means that surrounding vowels take a frontal quality, especially alif and fatHa, which sound like *bad* or *bet*.

LISTENING EXERCISE 3. 📀

LISTEN TO AND READ ALOUD WORDS CONTAINING س .

حَسَدَ   وَسْواس   سُبات   بَسَّ   سادات

WRITING 📀

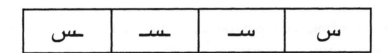

س is a connecting letter that is distinguished in print by its three "teeth." In handwriting, however, س is often written without its teeth, as a long straight line (this varies according to regional practice or personal preference). In either case, it takes a tail when written independently or in final position. Compare the printed and handwritten forms of the following:

درس   حسب   سبب

You will quickly become accustomed to reading س with its teeth in print. We suggest you learn to handwrite it without them so that you get accustomed to reading it that way, too. To write independent س , begin on the line and draw a very small hook, just enough to indicate the beginning of a letter. Continue into the long, flat body, then dip below the line into the tail, **making sure that it comes all the way back up to the line in a full semicircle.** Watch Professor El-Shinnawi and copy the examples:

Initial ـسـ is written just like independent س but without the tail. The body of connected ـسـ merges into the connecting segment so that the two are indistinguishable, so make sure to **lengthen** the body of the letter. Copy the word سَبَب (reason):

When ـسـ is connected from a previous letter, the connecting segment and the body of the letter are indistinguishable and **there is no hook on the beginning**, so that the connecting segment and the letter together form a single flat line like this: _____ . The body of this toothless س must be long enough to distinguish it from a connecting segment. **Remember** when reading **handwriting** that a long flat line _____ represents ـسـ (but in **print**, a long flat line without teeth does **not** represent ـسـ). Copy this connecting handwritten form in the word حِساب (arithmetic):

Final ـس is written with its tail, which **must come all the way back up to the line** (lest it be mistaken for ـر). Copy final ـس in the colloquial word بَسّ (that's all, enough):

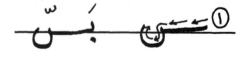

DRILL 4. DVD
DICTATION.

1. _____   3. _____   5. _____

2. _____   4. _____   6. _____

دودج سبيريت

ش

shiin

This letter corresponds to the sound *sh* in *shoe*.

LISTENING EXERCISE 4. DVD

LISTEN TO AND READ ALOUD WORDS CONTAINING ش .

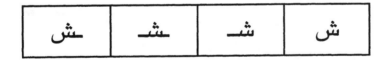

رَشّاش   حَشيش   باشا   بَشير   شِبْر

WRITING DVD

ـش	ـشـ	شـ	ش

The letter ش is a connector, and its shapes match those of س , except that this letter takes three dots above. In handwriting, ش is written without its teeth (like س) and the three dots are connected in a caret (just like those of ث). Practice writing independent ش by watching the DVD and copying the example:

_____

_____

Practice initial ﺸ by copying شـيـخ (*sheikh*):

_____

_____

Copy medial and final ـشـ in حَشيش (*grass*):

_____

_____

DRILL 5. *DVD*
DICTATION.

1. _____ 4. _____

2. _____ 5. _____

3. _____ 6. _____

DRILL 6. *DVD*
WRITE THE NAMES YOU HEAR. (NAMES 1-4 ARE FEMALE AND 5-8 ARE MALE. THE TWO FEMALE NAMES THAT END IN AN *A* SOUND ARE SPELLED WITH ALIF.)

1. _____ 5. _____

2. _____ 6. _____

3. _____ 7. _____

4. _____ 8. _____

Saad

This letter represents the emphatic counterpart of س . Pronounce س aloud, and note the position of your tongue: it should be toward the front of and close to the roof of the mouth. Now, starting at the back of your teeth, move your tongue back along the roof of your mouth. You will find a bony ridge just behind the teeth, before the upward curve of the roof. Put your tongue against this ridge. The rest of your tongue will drop lower inside your mouth. The emphatic or velarized consonants in Arabic are pronounced by placing the end of your tongue in this spot and dropping the rest of the tongue as low as you can. **Remember:** this and other emphatic consonants deepen the sound of surrounding vowels, most noticeably alif and fatHa, which sound like *a* in *father* and *u* in *but*. Pay attention to the sound of all vowels near these emphatic letters, because **the quality of the vowels gives the clearest indication of emphatic consonants.** Go back to the alphabet chart and click alternately on س and ص until you can hear the difference clearly.

LISTENING EXERCISE 5. 💿

LISTEN TO AND PRONOUNCE WORDS WITH ص , PAYING PARTICULAR ATTENTION TO THE SURROUNDING VOWELS.

حِصّة   صُوَر   صَباح   صار   صاد

WRITING 💿

ـص	ـصـ	صـ	ص

The letter ص is a connector, and it retains the same basic shape in both print and handwriting. There are two essential points to keep in mind when writing ص : (a) the loop must be big and oval-shaped, and (b) there must be a small "tooth" after the loop. To write independent ص , start on the line and make a big loop up and back to your right, then swing down and close it. Without stopping, make the tooth and then drop well below the line to make the tail. The tail of ص is the same shape as that of س and **must come all the way back up to the line.** Watch the DVD and copy:

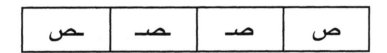

Initial ‏صـ‎ is written the same way, without the tail. After making the tooth, continue on to the connecting segment. Copy ‏صَبـاح‎ (*morning*):

‏صباح‎

To write ‏ـصـ‎ connected from a previous letter, draw the connecting segment to the starting point of the loop, the same point at which you started in initial position, then follow the same steps as above. Copy, following the arrows:

Practice by copying the word ‏تَصْوير‎ (*photography*):

‏تَصْوير تَصْوير‎

Final ‏ـص‎ is connected the same way as medial ‏ـصـ‎ and ends with a final tail the same shape as the tail of ‏س‎. Practice by copying ‏شَـخْـص‎ (*person*):

‏شخص‎

LISTEN TO AND REPEAT THE FOLLOWING PAIRS OF WORDS CONTRASTING س AND ص . NOTICE THAT THE EMPHATIC QUALITY OF ص DEEPENS THE SOUND OF SURROUNDING VOWELS. LISTENING TO VOWEL QUALITY IS THE EASIEST WAY TO DISTINGUISH BETWEEN س AND ص.

أَصبَح / أَسبَح   صاح / ساح   صين / سين   صُوَر / سُوَر   حَصَد / حَسَد

DRILL 7. 📀

READ THESE WORDS ALOUD WITH THE DVD, PAYING ATTENTION TO THE DIFFERENCE BETWEEN س AND ص :

1. (a) سارَ   (b) صارَ   4. (a) سَبْر   (b) صَبْر

2. (a) ساس   (b) صاص   5. (a) خَسّ   (b) خَصّ

3. (a) أَسير   (b) أَصير   6. (a) سَدَّت   (b) صَدَّت

DRILL 8. 📀

LISTEN TO THE WORDS ON DVD AND WRITE THE LETTER YOU HEAR IN THE BLANK. REMEMBER TO LISTEN FOR VOWEL QUALITY TO HELP YOU DISTINGUISH BETWEEN س AND ص .

1. حابِ ــ   5. ا ـــ دَرُ

2. رِي ــ بَ   6. تي ـــوْ ــ

3. ـــ بَ   7. بَحَ ـــ أ

4. دُر ـــ تَـ   8. دَ ـــ حَ

DRILL 9. 📀

YOU WILL HEAR TWELVE WORDS; EACH HAS EITHER س OR ص . WRITE THE LETTER THAT CORRESPONDS TO THE SOUND YOU HEAR:

1. _____   4. _____   7. _____   10. _____

2. _____   5. _____   8. _____   11. _____

3. _____   6. _____   9. _____   12. _____

DRILL 10. 📀
DICTATION.

1. _____   3. _____   5. _____

2. _____   4. _____   6. _____

ض

Daad

This letter represents the emphatic counterpart of د. To pronounce ض, place your tongue in the same position as you did to say ص and try to say د; the result will be ض. Remember that ض is an emphatic consonant that deepens the quality of surrounding vowels, especially alif and fatHa. Use the alphabet chart to contrast د and ض and practice aloud.

LISTENING EXERCISE 7. 📀

LISTEN TO AND READ ALOUD WORDS CONTAINING ض.

رِياض   حَضَرَ   خَضٌّ   ضَباب   ضاد

WRITING 📀

ض	ضـ	ـضـ	ـض

ض is a connector, and is written just like ص except that it takes one dot above. Watch Professor El-Shinnawi and follow the same steps you did for writing ص. Practice writing the independent form:

ض ضْ

Practice initial ضـ by copying the name of the letter, ضاد. Remember to give connecting ضـ its tooth:

ضاد ضْ

Now practice medial ـضـ by copying أخضـر (green):

أخضر

Practice final ـض in بَيْض (eggs):

بَيْض

LISTENING EXERCISE 8. 📀

LISTEN TO AND REPEAT THE PAIRS OF WORDS CONTRASTING د AND ض .

دَرْب / ضَرْب   دَبّ / ضَبّ   خَدّ / خَضّ   رِيادة / رِياضة   دالّ / ضالّ

DRILL 11. 📀

MARK **X** FOR EACH WORD IN WHICH YOU HEAR ض :

1. _____	4. _____	7. _____	10. _____
2. _____	5. _____	8. _____	11. _____
3. _____	6. _____	9. _____	12. _____

DRILL 12. 📀

READ THE FOLLOWING PAIRS OF WORDS ALOUD WITH THE **DVD**, PAYING PARTICULAR ATTENTION TO THE DIFFERENCE BETWEEN د AND ض :

1. (a) رَدّ   (b) رَضّ   5. (a) دَرْبي   (b) ضَرْبي

2. (a) يَدُرّ   (b) يَضُرّ   6. (a) دَجَرَ   (b) ضَجَرَ

3. (a) تَحَدَّرَت   (b) تَحَضَّرَت   7. (a) حَرَّدَت   (b) حَرَّضَت

4. (a) بيد   (b) بيض   8. (a) دَرَّس   (b) ضَرَّس

- 62 -

Drill 13. DVD

YOU WILL HEAR TWELVE WORDS, EACH CONTAINING EITHER د OR ض . WRITE THE LETTER THAT CORRESPONDS TO THE SOUND YOU HEAR:

1. ____   4. ____   7. ____   10. ____

2. ____   5. ____   8. ____   11. ____

3. ____   6. ____   9. ____   12. ____

Drill 14. DVD

LISTEN TO THE WORDS ON DVD AND WRITE THE LETTER YOU HEAR IN THE BLANK:

1. باب ____   4. أ ____ رِب   7. تَ ____ ريس

2. تَحْري ____   5. ____ حْر   8. أ ____ رار

3. تُبي ____   6. سر ____ ي   9. تَ ____ ا ريس

Drill 15. DVD

CONNECT THE LETTERS TO FORM WORDS. THEN LISTEN TO THE WORDS ON DVD AND WRITE IN THE SHORT VOWELS YOU HEAR.

1. _____ = ر + و + ب + ص

2. _____ = ي + ب + ا + ب + ش

3. _____ = ر+ ا + ر + س + أ

4. _____ = ر + ي + د + ص + ت

5. _____ = د + ا + ر + ي + ت + س + ا

6. _____ = خ + ي + ر + ا + و + ص

7. _____ = ت + ا + و + ر + ض + خ

8. _____ = ب + ا + ر + ا + و + ش

9. _____ = ت + ا + ر + ا + ش + ا

10. _____ = ح + ا + ب + ص

11. _____ = ي + ر + و + ص

12. _____ = ر + ي + ص + ا + ر + ص

13. _____ = ت + ض + ر + ض + ر + ت

14. _____ = ت + ا + ص + صّ + خ + ت

- 63 -

DRILL 16. DVD
DICTATION.

1. _____   6. _____

2. _____   7. _____

3. _____   8. _____

4. _____   9. _____

5. _____   10. _____

DRILL 17. DVD
READ THE FOLLOWING WORDS ALOUD:

رَصاص	أَبْيَض	خَضْراء	أَخْضَر
شاي	شَراب	تَسْيير	أَسْوَد
تَشْريح	صُراخ	شِتاء	شَجَر
صَواب	صَوْت	صَباح	سَبْت
إخْراج	ضَحايا	حَواجِز	صاحِب
تَدْريس	ضَوْء	صَحيح	أَصْحاب
زِيارات	حُجَج	حِساب	ذُباب

من جريدة الشرق الاوسط، ١٩٩٢

ARABIC SIGNS DVD
READ THE ARABIC SIGNS ON DVD WITH YOUR TEACHER. SOUND OUT THE WORDS AND NAMES—WHICH ONES DO YOU RECOGNIZE?

VOCABULARY 📀

GO TO YOUR DVD TO LISTEN TO AND LEARN THESE WORDS (THEY INCLUDE THE WORDS FOR *GOOD, YOUNG PEOPLE, YOUNG WOMEN, BUS, MORNING, TEA,* AND *LESSON*):

صَباح   شابّات   شَباب   شاي   دَرس   جَيِّد   أوتوبيس

DRILL 18.

MATCH THE PICTURES WITH THE WORDS YOU LEARNED.

- 65 -

GENDER

In the video scenes, you have heard people address and refer to men and women differently: a male professor is addressed or referred to as *duktuur* and a female as *duktuura*. In Arabic, all nouns are either masculine or feminine. That means there is no word for *it* in Arabic, so you must use *he* or *she* depending on what you are talking about. Start practicing this now by thinking of the nouns you learn by their **Arabic** pronoun: *huwa* (he) or *hiya* (she).

Within the category of people, masculine nouns refer to males. To refer to females, these masculine nouns take a feminine ending pronounced *a*. For example, masculine *ustaadh* أستــاز becomes feminine *ustaadha*. Within the category of inanimate beings or things, each noun has its own gender, which does not change. Masculine words usually end in a consonant, and feminine nouns almost always end in the feminine *a*. There are a few exceptions whose gender must be memorized, but in most cases, you can tell by hearing or reading a word what its gender is.

You have learned two sets of nouns in which the feminine ending is pronounced with a "t" sound: صاحبي / صاحبتي and حبيبي / حبيبتي. You will learn about the feminine ending in the next chapter.

الوحدة الخامسة
UNIT FIVE

غ   ع   ظ   ط   ة

This unit presents the feminine ending ة and the next four consonants in the alphabet.

ة

taa marbuuTa

This symbol is not considered a part of the Arabic alphabet because its function is primarily grammatical. It can only occur at the end of nouns and adjectives. This letter is called *taa marbuuTa*, meaning *the tied* ت , and it almost always indicates feminine gender (the rare exceptions to this rule will be noted as they arise). As its name and form indicate, ة is related to the letter ت , and sometimes it is pronounced as ت (you will learn this rule later). At other times it is not pronounced as ت , but **the fatHa vowel that always precedes ة is always pronounced.** In spoken Arabic, a fatHa at the end of a word will almost always indicate ة . **Remember:** when you hear a noun that ends with a fatHa sound, you can usually assume that it is feminine, and spelled with a ة .

LISTENING EXERCISE 1. 📀

LISTEN TO AND READ ALOUD WORDS ENDING IN ة :

صورة   شَجَرة   زوجة   وَردة   أُستاذة

DRILL 1. 📀

LISTEN TO THE WORDS ON **DVD** AND MARK **X** FOR EACH WORD YOU HEAR THAT ENDS IN ة :

1. _____   4. _____   7. _____

2. _____   5. _____   8. _____

3. _____   6. _____   9. _____

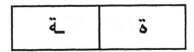

ــة	ة

Since ة only occurs in word-final position, it has only two shapes: one that follows connecting letters and one that follows nonconnectors. In print, the two dots appear separately, as you can see, but in handwriting, they are usually drawn together as a short horizontal bar (just like the dots of ت and ي). To write ة after a nonconnecting letter, start above the line at the top of the letter and draw the loop down to your right and back up. Watch Ustaadh El-Shinnawi write ة , then copy the word أستاذة :

أُسْـتَاذة

To write ة connected to a previous letter, start at the connecting segment, draw the right side of the loop up into a point, then swing back down to your left to close the loop. The shape of this loop is usually lopsided and not as round as when ة is written alone, and individual handwriting styles vary. Copy the word زَوجة *(wife)* as shown:

زَوجة

Now copy and sound out the following words containing ة .

خارِجيّة   زَوجة   جَريدة   سَيِّدة   دِراسة

ط

Taa

This letter represents the emphatic counterpart of ت . To pronounce it, put the tip of your tongue up against the bony ridge behind your teeth on the roof of your mouth, the same position used for ض , and drop your tongue low in your mouth. Try to say *t* holding this position—the result will be ط . The difference in pronunciation between ط and ت parallels that between ض and د . **Remember:** ط is an emphatic sound that deepens the quality of surrounding vowels. Go back to the alphabet chart and contrast ت and ط until you can hear the difference clearly.

LISTENING EXERCISE 2. *DVD*

LISTEN TO AND READ ALOUD WORDS CONTAINING ط .

طَبيب   طالِب   رُطوبة   بَطّيخ   ضـابِط   شُـبـاط

WRITING *DVD*

ط	ط	ط	ط

ط is a connector and is written in two separate steps. Follow Ustaadh El-Shinnawi's steps closely and do **not** write ط by beginning at the top with the downstroke, otherwise you will not be able to connect this letter properly. The loop that forms the body is written in one motion, connected to the rest of the word, and the vertical line is written afterwards, much like crossing the *t* in cursive English.

To write ط independently, start on the line and make the loop first. It should be large, oblong, and fall along the line lengthwise, as you see. The final step in writing ط is the downstroke. After forming the loop, pick up your pen and draw this stroke as you do the alif, from the top down. Most people write the downstroke at or near the left end of the loop. Write independent ط as shown:

To write a word beginning with ط , begin exactly as you did above, and continue on into a smooth connecting segment without stopping. **Unlike ص and ض , ط does not have a tooth** between the loop and the connecting segment. Copy طَـبِـيـب (*doctor*):

طبيب طبيب

When writing ط in medial position, start from the connecting segment, continue along the line, and **without** lifting the pen, loop backwards and around to the line again to continue on to the next letter. Do not stop to write the downstroke until you have finished writing the body of the word. Like dotting the *i* or crossing the *t* in English script, this is done at the end, as the example shows. Copy the word سَطْر (*line*):

Now copy the following words containing ط :

(*handwriting*) خَطّ   (*he flies*) يَطِير   (*veterinarian*) طَبِيب بَيْطَرِي

Remember that, since ط is an emphatic letter, it affects the quality of surrounding vowels, so that alif and fatHa sound like *a* in *father* and *u* in *but*.

LISTENING EXERCISE 3. DVD

LISTEN TO THE PAIRS OF WORDS CONTRASTING ت AND ط :

تاب / طاب   شَتّ / شَطّ   رَتَّبَ / رَطَّبَ   سَتْر / سَطْر   حَتّ / حَطّ

- 70 -

DRILL 2. *DVD*

LISTEN TO THE PAIRS OF WORDS ON DVD AND CIRCLE THE LETTER OF THE WORD THAT CONTAINS ط :

1. a   b   6. a   b
2. a   b   7. a   b
3. a   b   8. a   b
4. a   b   9. a   b
5. a   b   10. a   b

DRILL 3. *DVD*

MARK X FOR EACH WORD IN WHICH YOU HEAR ط :

1. ____   3. ____   5. ____   7. ____   9. ____

2. ____   4. ____   6. ____   8. ____   10. ____

DRILL 4. *DVD*

READ THE FOLLOWING PAIRS OF WORDS WITH THE DVD, PAYING SPECIAL ATTENTION TO ت AND ط AND THE QUALITY OF THE SURROUNDING VOWELS:

1. (a) أَوْتار   (b) أَوْطار   5. (a) وَتَّرَ   (b) وَطَّدَ
2. (a) رَتيب   (b) رَطيب   6. (a) أَتْـرَحَ   (b) أَطْـرَحَ
3. (a) وَتْـوات   (b) وَطْـواط   7. (a) تَـيّار   (b) طَـيّار
4. (a) بَتّ   (b) بَطّ   8. (a) توب   (b) طوب

DRILL 5. *DVD*

LISTEN TO THE WORDS ON DVD AND WRITE THE LETTER YOU HEAR IN THE BLANK:

1. حَـ ـ ـب   4. خَـ ـ   7. دُسـ ـ ـور

2. راب ـ ـة   5. ـ بْشورة   8. شَـ ـ ـاء

3. ـ ـزْخَر   6. سُـ ـ ـور   9. بُـحـ ـ

DRILL 6. *DVD*

DICTATION.

1. _____   3. _____   5. _____

2. _____   4. _____   6. _____

DHaa

This letter represents the emphatic counterpart of ذ . Place your tongue in the same position as you did for ط, and try to say ذ . The tip of your tongue should be between your teeth, but the rest of your tongue should remain in the same position as for ط, low in the mouth. **Remember:** ظ is an emphatic sound that deepens the quality of surrounding vowels. Go to the alphabet chart on your DVD and watch and listen to ذ and ظ .

LISTENING EXERCISE 4. *DVD*
LISTEN TO THE WORDS ON DVD AND REPEAT, WITH ATTENTION TO VOWEL QUALITY.

ظُهور   حَظّ   شَظِيّة   ظالِم   أبو ظَبي

WRITING *DVD*

ظ	ظ	ظ	ظ

ظ is a connector and is written like ط in all positions, with the addition of one dot above the body. Watch the DVD and follow the arrows to write independent ظ :

When writing initial and medial ظ , **do not stop** to "cross" and dot ظ until you have finished writing the skeleton of the word. Copy the name of the Arab Emirate, أبو ظَبي , as shown:

أبوظبي أبوظبي

Copy and sound out the following words containing ظ :

حَظّ (luck)   بوظة (ice cream)   ظَبْي (gazelle)

_____

_____

LISTENING EXERCISE 5. 💿

LISTEN TO THE CONTRAST BETWEEN ذ AND ظ IN THE PAIRS OF WORDS AND REPEAT.

نَظَر / نَذَر   ظَلّ / ذَلّ   حَظَر / حَذَر   ظَنّ / ذَنَب   ذال / ظاء

DRILL 7. 💿

LISTEN TO THE PAIRS OF WORDS AND CIRCLE THE LETTER OF THE WORD THAT CONTAINS ظ :

1.	a	b		6.	a	b
2.	a	b		7.	a	b
3.	a	b		8.	a	b
4.	a	b		9.	a	b
5.	a	b		10.	a	b

LISTENING EXERCISE 6. 💿

RECOGNITION OF ث, ذ, ض, AND ظ. LISTEN TO THESE WORDS TO REVIEW THESE SOUNDS:

1. (a) ظَبْي   (b) ضابِط   (c) ذابَت   (d) ثابِت

2. (a) حَظَر   (b) حَضَر   (c) حَذَر   (d) حَثّ

3. (a) بَظّ   (b) بَضّ   (c) بَذّ   (d) بَثّ

DRILL 8. 💿

YOU WILL HEAR TEN WORDS. FOR EACH, CIRCLE THE SOUND YOU HEAR:

1.	ظ	ض	ذ	ث	6.	ظ	ض	ذ	ث
2.	ظ	ض	ذ	ث	7.	ظ	ض	ذ	ث
3.	ظ	ض	ذ	ث	8.	ظ	ض	ذ	ث
4.	ظ	ض	ذ	ث	9.	ظ	ض	ذ	ث
5.	ظ	ض	ذ	ث	10.	ظ	ض	ذ	ث

READ THE WORDS ALOUD WITH THE DVD, PAYING ATTENTION TO ظ , ذ , ث :

	(a)	(b)	(c)
1.	ثَبَتَ	ذُبـاب	ظَبَيْـة
2.	حُثّي	حوذي	حَظّي
3.	يَحُثُّ	يَحذو	يَحظو
4.	أثَّرَ	حَذَّرَ	حَظَّرَ

LISTEN TO THE WORDS AND WRITE THE LETTER YOU HEAR IN THE BLANK:

1. ــبي	4. أ ـــ واب	7. حِـ ـــ اء	10. جَـ ـــ وة
2. تَحْـ ـــ ير	5. أ ـــ رياء	8. إ ـــ بات	11. حَـ ـــ يّة
3. حَـ ـــ	6. ــبت	9. ــبْط	12. بُـ ـــ ور

DICTATION.

1. _____   3. _____   5. _____   7. _____

2. _____   4. _____   6. _____   8. _____

READ THE FOLLOWING PAIRS OF NOUNS ALOUD. WHAT CAN YOU GUESS ABOUT THE RELATIONSHIP BETWEEN THE WORDS IN EACH PAIR?

حِزْب أحْزاب	دار دور	ضَرورة ضَرورات
أسْتاذ أساتذة	صورة صُوَر	طَبيب أطِبّاء
واجِب واجِبات	جُثّة جُثَث	شَيْخ شُيوخ
حارة حارات	أُستاذة أُستاذات	حاجّ حُجّاج
طَيْر طُيور	سَيّارة سَيّارات	طَبيبة طَبيبات
ظَبْيـة ظِباء	ضابِط ضُبّاط	يَخْت يُخوت

$$\boxed{\text{ع}}$$

ᶜayn

We now come to one of the most distinctive sounds in Arabic: ع . When pronounced correctly, ع has its own unique beauty and can be a very expressive sound. The degree to which ع is emphasized differs slightly from one dialect area to another; in the Gulf and some areas of North Africa, it is pronounced with a greater constricting of the muscles and has a more powerful sound. It is not difficult to pronounce, but you need to exercise your throat muscles, the same ones that you use to pronounce ح . You should still be doing the exercises you learned above for ح , in which you constrict your throat muscles as if you were blocking off the air passage from the inside. You can feel this by putting your hand on your throat. Say ح , and feel the muscles contract. Now pronounce the same sound and voice it, that is, instead of a breathy sound, make a deep, throaty sound. Keep your hand on your throat so that you can feel your muscles contracting. Also, if you bend your head down so that your chin rests on your chest, you will be able to feel and hear what you are doing more easily. Use the alphabet chart to listen and watch the pronunciation of ع .

LISTENING EXERCISE 7. 📀

LISTEN TO AND READ ALOUD THE WORDS CONTAINING ع IN VARIOUS POSITIONS.

دَع   رَعْي   ساعة   يَعود   عاد   عَيْب   عَرَبي

It is helpful to put your hand to your throat so that you can feel the muscles contract every time you say ع for the next few weeks, until you are accustomed to the sound. ع is a very important sound in Arabic, and you must learn to say it properly in order to be understood. The more you practice now, the sooner ع will become natural for you.

WRITING 📀

عـ	ـعـ	ـع	ع

ع is a connecting letter whose shape varies somewhat depending on its position. Watch Ustaadh El-Shinnawi as he writes the various shapes of this letter and imitate his motions. In independent and initial positions, the common element is a c-shape that rests on the line. As an independent letter, it takes a tail, when connected to a following letter, it

leads into a connecting segment as shown. Practice writing and pronouncing independent ع as the examples show:

ع   غ

Copy the word شارع (*street*):

شارع   شارع

Practice connecting ع to a following letter by copying ساعة (*clock*):

ساعة

When ـع is connected from a previous letter in medial and final positions, the body of the letter becomes a closed loop. Rather than a c-shape, the left side of the body comes to a point, while the right side may be pointed as well or slightly curved. In some calligraphy styles, the body appears filled in, but most people write it open as the example shows. Practice writing the shape of medial ـع :

ـعـ   ـعـ

Now copy بَعيد (*far*):

بَعيد   بَعيد

- 76 -

In final position, ـع reassumes its tail. Practice by copying أربع (*four*):

أَرْبَع

LISTENING EXERCISE 8. *DVD*

LISTEN TO THE FOLLOWING PAIRS OF WORDS AND REPEAT, PAYING ATTENTION TO THE PRONUNCIATION OF ء
AND ع. REMEMBER THAT ء IS A SOUND YOU PRODUCE NATURALLY, WITHOUT EFFORT. SAY *UH-OH* BEFORE
PRONOUNCING ء, AND PUT YOUR HAND ON YOUR THROAT WHEN PRONOUNCING ع.

أَطَّر / عَطَّر   أَبَد / عَبَد   أَسير / عَسير   تَأَثَّرَ / تَعَثَّرَ   وَأَدَ / وَعَدَ

DRILL 13. *DVD*

READ THE FOLLOWING PAIRS OF WORDS ALOUD WITH THE DVD, PAYING SPECIAL ATTENTION TO THE DIFFERENCE
BETWEEN ع AND ء :

1. (a) أَيَّدَت (b) عَيَّدَت	6. (a) أزيز (b) عَزيز
2. (a) إبْرة (b) عِبْرة	7. (a) جَأْجَأَ (b) جَعْجَعَ
3. (a) تَعَطَّرَ (b) تَأَطَّرَ	8. (a) شاءَ (b) شاعَ
4. (a) رَأْي (b) رَعْي	9. (a) صَدَأَ (b) صَدَعَ
5. (a) جاءَت (b) جاعَت	10. (a) أَجْزَأَت (b) أَجْزَعَت

DRILL 14. *DVD*

YOU WILL HEAR NINE WORDS. FOR EACH, CIRCLE THE SOUND YOU HEAR:

1. ع ء	4. ع ء	7. ع ء
2. ع ء	5. ع ء	8. ع ء
3. ع ء	6. ع ء	9. ع ء

Drill 15. DVD

LISTEN TO THE WORDS ON DVD AND WRITE THE LETTER YOU HEAR IN THE BLANK:

ـطِر ــ .1   ـحِبّ ــ .4   صَـ ــ ب .7

رَـ ــ د .2   ـودِي ــ .5   ثَـ ــ رِي .8

شارِ ــ .3   دَـ ــ وات .6   تَسـ ــ يِر .9

Drill 16. DVD
DICTATION.

1. _____   5. _____

2. _____   6. _____

3. _____   7. _____

4. _____   8. _____

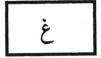

<u>ghayn</u>

This letter is pronounced like a voiced خ . Think of the correspondence between the sounds *k* (*kite*) and *g* (*game*): *k* is unvoiced and *g* is voiced. Pronounce *k* and *g* several times, paying attention to how your voice changes when you say *g*. Now say خ several times, then voice it. Alternatively, you may think of غ as similar to the sound you make when gargling. Gargle for a minute and pay attention to the muscles that you use. غ is pronounced using these same muscles in similar fashion. Use the alphabet chart to watch and listen to غ, and practice until you can say it easily.

LISTENING EXERCISE 9. DVD

LISTEN TO AND READ ALOUD THE WORDS CONTAINING غ IN VARIOUS POSITIONS.

غَريب   بَغداد   صَغير   طاغي   تَبغ   غُربة   غُربة

غ	ـغـ	ـغـ	غ

غ is a connector and has the same shapes as ع , except that it takes a single dot above. Watch the DVD and copy independent غ as shown:

غ غ

Now write صاغ (*piaster*, an Egyptian coin):

صاغ صاغ

Initial ـغ connects to a following letter as shown. Practice writing and pronouncing the word غَبي (*stupid*). Do not stop to dot until you have finished writing the entire word:

غبي غ

Medial ـغـ is written just like medial ـغـ . Copy and pronounce بَغداد :

بغداد غ

Final غ assumes the long tail. Practice by copying and saying تبغ (tobacco):

تَبْغ   يَخ   تَبْغ   ①   ②

LISTENING EXERCISE 10. DVD

LISTEN TO AND REPEAT THESE WORDS CONTRASTING THE SOUNDS غ AND خ :

يَغيب / يَخيب   غَضّ / خَضّ   يُغَرِّب/يُخَرِّب   تَغُصّ /تَخُصّ

DRILL 17. DVD

YOU WILL HEAR NINE WORDS. CIRCLE THE LETTER CORRESPONDING TO THE SOUND YOU HEAR:

1.	خ	غ	4.	خ	غ	7.	خ	غ
2.	خ	غ	5.	خ	غ	8.	خ	غ
3.	خ	غ	6.	خ	غ	9.	خ	غ

DRILL 18. DVD

READ THESE PAIRS OF WORDS ALOUD WITH THE DVD, WITH ATTENTION TO غ AND خ :

1. (a) تَغريب (b) تَخريب   6. (a) رَغْوة (b) رَخْوة

2. (a) يَشغُر (b) يَشخُر   7. (a) غَرير (b) خَرير

3. (a) غَيْري (b) خَيْري   8. (a) تَغُطّ (b) تَخُطّ

4. (a) بَغْت (b) بَخْت   9. (a) غَبَّط (b) خَبَّط

5. (a) غَيْبة (b) خَيْبة   10. (a) غَضير (b) خَضير

DRILL 19. DVD

LISTEN TO THE WORDS ON DVD AND WRITE THE LETTER YOU HEAR IN THE BLANK:

1. صَـــ ـــ ـير   4. شَـــ ـــ ب   7. سُـــ ـــ رية

2. تَـــ ـــ يُر   5. ـــ ياطة   8. تَـــ ـرُجي

3. ـــ ـزّة   6. طا ـــ ية   9. ضَـــ ط ـــ ط

DRILL 20.
CONNECT THE LETTERS TO FORM WORDS AND SOUND THEM OUT.

8. ــــــــــــ = ة + يّ + بِ + رْ + غَ   1. ــــــــــــ = ة + ح + ا + ر + صَ

9. ــــــــــــ = ء + ا + بّ + طِ + أ   2. ــــــــــــ = ت + ا + ر + يُّ + غَ + تَ

10. ــــــــــــ = ا + ي + ا + ظ + شَ   3. ــــــــــــ = د + ي + ع + بَ

11. ــــــــــــ = ي + ح + ا + و + ضَ   4. ــــــــــــ = ة + يّ + صِ + خْ + شَ

12. ــــــــــــ = ر + ي + غِ + صْ + تَ   5. ــــــــــــ = ب + رَ + غْ + تَ + سْ + اِ

13. ــــــــــــ = ص + صُّ + خَ + تَ   6. ــــــــــــ = ي + د + و + ر + طُ

14. ــــــــــــ = غ + سْ + رُ   7. ــــــــــــ = ض + ا + ر + تَ + غْ + اِ

DRILL 21. 📀
YOU WILL HEAR NINE WORDS. CIRCLE THE WORD YOU HEAR IN EACH ROW:

1.   غَرَّب   خَرَّب   جَرَّب   حَرَّب

2.   ضَرَّس   دَرَّس   دَرَز   دَرَس

3.   أَسبَح   اطْبَع   إصْبَع   أصبَح

4.   ذاع   صاع   ضاع   شاع

5.   صَغير   سَرير   صَرير   شِرّير

6.   حُثّ   جِصّ   حِصّ   حِسّ

7.   حَذَر   حَصَر   حَظَر   حَضَر

8.   ضَبي   سَبي   صَبي   ظَبي

9.   غَبَّر   عِبَر   عَبَّر   أبَرّ

DRILL 22. 📀
DICTATION.

1. _____   6. _____

2. _____   7. _____

3. _____   8. _____

4. _____   9. _____

5. _____   10. _____

Vocabulary DVD

Go to your DVD to listen to and learn these words (they include *watch/clock*, *street*, *teacher/professor*, *Mr.*, *Mrs.*, *friend(s)*, *car*, *Arab*, *happy*, and *wide/spacious*):

صاحب ، صاحبة ، أصحاب	سيد ، سيدة	أستاذ ، أستاذة
شارِع	سَيّارة	ساعة
سعيد ، سعيدة	واسِع / واسعة	عَرَبي / عربية

Listen to and learn these adjectives:

DIFFICULT, HARD	صَعْب / صعبة
GOOD, KIND (OF PEOPLE), GOOD, TASTY (OF FOOD)	طيِّب / طيِّبة
ASTONISHING, STRANGE	عجيب / عجيبة
STRANGE, ODD	غريب / غريبة

DRILL 23.

Match the words you learned with the pictures:

 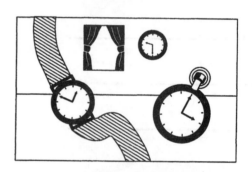

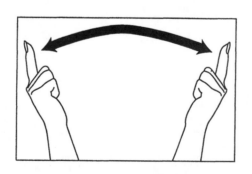

DRILL 24.

MATCH THE NOUNS AND ADJECTIVES YOU HAVE LEARNED IN UNITS 1-5 TO FORM INDEFINITE NOUN-ADJECTIVE
PHRASES AS THE EXAMPLES SHOW. MAKE PHRASES THAT ARE MEANINGFUL TO YOU: THINK OF A REAL CONTEXT
IN WHICH YOU MIGHT SAY SUCH A THING. REMEMBER TO MAKE THE GENDER OF THE ADJECTIVE AGREE WITH
THAT OF THE NOUN (THE GENDER OF NOUNS DOES NOT CHANGE, EXCEPT THOSE REFERRING TO HUMAN BEINGS,
ACCORDING TO HUMAN GENDER). REMEMBER ALSO THAT IN ARABIC, THE NOUN ALWAYS PRECEDES THE
ADJECTIVE.

a new teacher/professor (female)   أُستاذة جديدة

a wide/spacious house   بَيت واسِـع

1. _____

2. _____

3. _____

4. _____

5. _____

6. _____

7. _____

8. _____

9. _____

10. _____

11. _____

12. _____

13. _____

14. _____

15. _____

16. _____

17. _____

18. _____

19. _____

20. _____

ARABIC SIGNS 📀

READ THE ARABIC SIGNS ON DVD WITH YOUR TEACHER. SOUND OUT THE WORDS AND NAMES—WHICH ONES DO YOU RECOGNIZE?

DIALOGUES 📀

WATCH SCENE 7 *Tasharrafnaa.*

CULTURE: FORMS OF ADDRESS

You have learned to use *HaDritak* (حَضـرتَك) and *HaDritik* (حَضـرتِك) for polite *you*. In addition, various titles are often used to address people politely. Some of the titles commonly used in Arabic are:

دُكـتـور / دُكـتـورة *duktuur / duktuura* (Dr.), used to address or refer to medical and academic professionals (whether or not they have a Ph.D.).

أُستاذ / أُستاذة *ustaadh / ustaadha* (literally, *teacher, professor*), used to address or refer to an educated person, white-collar employee, schoolteacher, etc. (You have heard the spoken Cairene pronunciation of this title in the dialogues: *Ustaaz* and *Ustaaza*. In the urban dialects of Egypt, Syria, and Lebanon, ذ may be pronounced as ز.)

سَيِّـد *sayyid* (**Mr.**), used in formal situations and correspondence to refer to or introduce people who have no professional title.

سَيِّـدة *sayyida* (**Mrs.**), and مَـدام *madaam*, used to address or refer to older and/or married women.

آنسة *aanisa* (**Miss**), used to address or refer to a young, unmarried woman.

These titles are followed by the person's first or full name (and not by the last name alone). When addressing someone directly, these titles are preceded by *yaa* (يا) (no English equivalent, signals to the person that she/he is being addressed):

yaa duktuur George!	يا دكتـور جورج!
yaa duktuura Aida!	يا دكتورة عايدة!
yaa ustaadh Abbas!	يا استاذ عبّاس!
yaa ustaadha Zeinab!	يا استاذة زَيْنَب!
yaa aanisa Samia!	يا آنسة سامية!

الوحدة السادسة
UNIT SIX

$$\boxed{\text{ل} \qquad \text{ك} \qquad \text{ق} \qquad \text{ف}}$$

In this unit you will learn four new consonants and more vocabulary.

faa

This letter is pronounced like English *f* as in *feather*.

LISTENING EXERCISE 1. *DVD*

Listen to and read aloud the words containing ف .

صُفوف　　عَفاف　　سَفيـر　　دَفْتَر　　فَريد　　فَرَح

WRITING *DVD*

ف	ف	ف	ف

ف is a connecting letter with a relatively stable shape. Its independent and final forms have a tail that is unusual in that it remains on the line rather than dipping below. To write independent ف , begin above the line and draw a small, flat loop around to your left, up, and down around. Keep the loop of ف small and just above the line, resting on a short "neck." Continue along the line into a small hook to finish the tail as Ustaaz El-Shinnawi does. Practice writing independent ف :

To write ‎فـ‎ in initial position, begin the same way and finish with a connecting segment into the next letter. Copy the name ‎فَريد‎ :

فَريد   فـ ②

The loop of medial ‎ـفـ‎ is small and oval (for example, it is **much** smaller than that of ‎ـط‎ , and has a different shape). Start from the connecting segment and loop up to your left and back around to the line and into the connecting segment, as the example shows:

ـفـ   ② ①

Write ‎صَفحة‎ (*page*). Remember to begin well above the line to leave room for the ‎ـح‎ :

صَفحة صَفحة

Final ‎ـف‎ combines the shape of the medial position with the tail of the independent ‎ف‎ . Copy ‎صَفّ‎ (*class*):

صَفّ ② ①

DRILL 1. DVD
DICTATION. WRITE THE NAMES YOU HEAR (1-6 ARE FEMALE, 7-12 ARE MALE).

1. _____   4. _____   7. _____   10. _____

2. _____   5. _____   8. _____   11. _____

3. _____   6. _____   9. _____   12. _____

ق

qaaf

This letter represents a new sound, the emphatic counterpart to *k*. Like the other emphatic sounds, it is pronounced with the tongue low in the mouth. It differs from them in that it is pronounced farther back in the throat, at the very back of the tongue. Take a minute to become more familiar with your throat muscles. Open your mouth and say *aah*, as if you were at the doctor. Your tongue should be flat in your mouth. Without raising your tongue, pull it back so that the base of your tongue closes off air by pulling back against the throat. At this point, you should not be able to breathe through your mouth, although it is wide open. Practice doing this first without making a sound. After performing this exercise several times, make a sound by releasing the air forcefully. The result will be the sound ق . Go to the alphabet chart and watch and listen to ق (you may want to go ahead and contrast it to the following letter, ك , which is its nonemphatic counterpart).

LISTENING EXERCISE 2. **DVD**
LISTEN TO ق **IN THE WORDS ON DVD AND REPEAT.**

فِراق بَرقوق شَفيق دَقيقة قارِب قاف

DRILL 2. **DVD**
MARK X FOR EACH WORD IN WHICH YOU HEAR ق :

1. _____   4. _____   7. _____

2. _____   5. _____   8. _____

3. _____   6. _____   9. _____

WRITING **DVD**

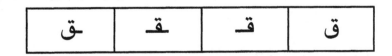

ق is a connector, and its shape is similar to that of ف in all positions, except that ق takes two dots above and a deep semicircle tail that drops well below the line like that of س and ص . The two dots above ق are usually run together in handwriting (like those of ت). To write independent ق , make the same loop you made for ف , then drop below the

line to draw the tail and **make sure to bring the tail all the way back up to the line.**
Watch Ustaaz El-Shinnawi on your DVD and copy the examples:

ق

Initial ـق is written just like initial ـف , but with two dots run together. Copy the example:

ق

Practice by writing قَـرِيـب (*near*). Do not stop to dot until you have finished writing the word:

قَرِيب قَرِيب

Medial ـقـ has the same shape and size as medial ـفـ , and is connected in the same way.
Practice by writing دَقِيقة (*minute*):

دَقِيقة دَقِيقة

Unlike final ـف , final ـق takes a tail that drops well below the line, just like that of س .
Make sure to bring it all the way back up to the line:

ق

Practice final ـق by writing بـرقـوق (*plum*):

بُرقوق بُرقوق

DRILL 3. 📀
DICTATION.

1. _____   4. _____

2. _____   5. _____

3. _____   6. _____

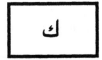

kaaf

This letter corresponds to English *k* as in *likewise*.[1] ك represents a familiar sound that takes no extra effort on your part. Take care to distinguish between it and ق, which is pronounced deep in the throat. **Remember:** ق is an emphatic letter that deepens the quality of surrounding vowels, whereas vowels surrounding ك are frontal.

LISTENING EXERCISE 3. 📀
LISTEN TO THE WORDS CONTAINING ك AND REPEAT.

رَكيـك   شُكوك   أَكيـد   حِكاية   دُكتور   كِتـاب

WRITING 📀

ـك	ـكـ	كـ	ك

As Ustaaz El-Shinnawi demonstrates on the DVD, ك is a connecting letter that has two distinct shapes, one in independent and final positions, and one in initial and medial

---

[1] Note that Arabic ك is never aspirated, that is , it has no "breathy" sound like that of *k* in *kite*.

- 90 -

positions. To write independent ك , start above the line at the top of the letter, draw straight down to the line, then curve and follow the line. Make a tiny hook at the end, then pick up your pen and draw a little hamza-like figure inside the angle. The shape of this mark, which may have originated as a miniature ك , may vary slightly in different scripts. Copy the example:

When ك is connected to a following letter, it has a cross bar on the top; however, this is written last, like the vertical bar of ط and ظ . To write initial ك , start as you do the independent form, drawing down to the line, then make a right angle and draw along it into a connecting segment. Note that the body of initial ك is not exactly perpendicular to the line on the paper—it may be slightly slanted or even curved, depending on individual style. After you finish writing the skeleton of the word, go back and "cross" the ك as shown (it does not matter if the bar is not exactly lined up, but keep it as close as possible). Copy initial ك , following the arrows:

Now practice writing initial ك in كَبِيـر (big):

Medial ـكـ is written like initial كـ, except that you must start from a connecting segment on the line and draw up, then trace the same line back down. (Again, the body does not have to be exactly perpendicular to the line, and its exact angle may vary somewhat.) Wait until you finish writing the word to draw the cross bar. Copy:

_____

_____

Practice writing medial ـكـ in فِكـرة (*idea*):

فِكرة   فِكرة

_____

_____

In certain artistic scripts and fonts, ـكـ takes a slightly different shape. Find ـكـ in each of these words:

اسكندرية   اسكندرية   دكتور   دكتور

كرايسلر

Final ـك is similar in shape to independent ك except that it is connected to the previous letter. Start from the connecting segment, draw a line up, roughly perpendicular to the line, then trace it back down, and give it a flat tail along the line (the same tail you draw for ـف). When you have finished writing, give it the little hamza-like mark as in the example:

ـك   ـك

_____

_____

Practice final ـك by writing شيك (*check*):

شيك شيك ᵊشيك

LISTENING EXERCISE 4. DVD

LISTEN TO THE DIFFERENCE BETWEEN ك AND ق IN THE PAIRS OF WORDS AND REPEAT:

شَقّ / شَكّ   باقِر / باكِر   قابوس / كابوس   رَقيق / رَكيك   قَدُّس / كَدُّس

DRILL 4. DVD

YOU WILL HEAR TWELVE WORDS. CIRCLE THE SOUND YOU HEAR IN EACH:

1. ق ك		5. ق ك		9. ق ك
2. ق ك		6. ق ك		10. ق ك
3. ق ك		7. ق ك		11. ق ك
4. ق ك		8. ق ك		12. ق ك

DRILL 5. DVD

READ THESE WORDS ALOUD WITH THE DVD, PAYING SPECIAL ATTENTION TO ك AND ق AND THE QUALITY OF THE SURROUNDING VOWELS:

	(a)	(b)			(a)	(b)
1.	كادَ	قادَ		6.	بَكَرَ	بَقَرَ
2.	شُكوك	شُقوق		7.	صَدَّكَ	صَدَّقَ
3.	كَسْوة	قَسْوة		8.	اِكتِفاء	اِقتِفاء
4.	كَدَّر	قَدَّر		9.	عِراك	عِراق
5.	حَبَك	حَبَق		10.	كُروش	قُروش

DRILL 6. DVD

WRITE THE LETTER THAT YOU HEAR IN EACH BLANK:

1. ــ ريب	4. ضَيِّ ـــ	7. حَظُّ ــ
2. بِطا ـــ ة	5. اِستشرا ـــ	8. فِ ـــ رة
3. صـ ــ ور	6. را ــ ص	9. سُ ـــ ر

DICTATION. WRITE THE NAMES YOU HEAR (1-6 ARE FEMALE, LISTEN FOR ة IN SOME; 7-12 ARE MALE):

1. _____   5. _____   9. _____

2. _____   6. _____   10. _____

3. _____   7. _____   11. _____

4. _____   8. _____   12. _____

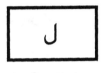

laam

This letter represents the sound of the Spanish or French *l*, that is, a frontal *l* in which the front part of the tongue is against the back of the teeth, and the tongue is high in the mouth. Americans tend to pronounce *l* with the tongue farther back and lower down in the mouth, resulting in a more emphatic sound than Arabic ل . Say the word *terrible* aloud, and notice that the position of your tongue when you say *ble* is similar to the position your tongue holds when you say ص , ض , and ط . To pronounce Arabic ل , hold the tip of your tongue against the back of your teeth at the roof of your mouth and keep your tongue as high and frontal as you can. Maintain this position while repeating the words you hear on DVD.

LISTENING EXERCISE 5. DVD

LISTEN TO AND REPEAT THE WORDS CONTAINING THE SOUND ل , KEEPING THE TIP OF YOUR TONGUE AGAINST THE BACK OF YOUR TEETH.

طَلَعَ   صَليب   طَويل   حُلول   عالية   حَليب   ليبيا

الله

The word for God in Arabic is *Allaah*. These two words are exact equivalents in meaning, and Christian Arabs and Jewish speakers of Arabic use الله for *God* just like Muslims do. The word الله is the only word in Arabic whose ل is emphatic in quality without influence from other emphatic consonants.

The word الله is used in many everyday expressions that have as much cultural content as religious. Listening Exercise 6 introduces you to some common expressions that include the word *Allaah* and their appropriate context. Note that الله is pronounced with a frontal ل if it is preceded by a kasra, as it is in the last expression below, *bismillaah*.

LISTEN TO THESE EXPRESSIONS CONTAINING THE WORD *Allaah*:

(expresses admiration or delight)	*Allaah!*	الله!
GOD WILLING	*in shaa'Allaah*	إن شاءَ الله
(used when praising or admiring)	*maa shaa'Allaah*	ما شاءَ الله!
THERE IS NO GOD BUT GOD (said upon hearing bad news)	*laa ilaaha illa Allaah*	لا إله إلاّ الله
MAY GOD HAVE MERCY ON HIM (=May he rest in peace)	*Allaah yirHamuh*	الله يرحَمُه
IN THE NAME OF GOD (said before or upon beginning something)	*bismillaah*	بِسْم الله

WRITING *DVD*

ل	ـلـ	ـل	ل

ل is a connecting letter. The shapes of ل are similar to those of ك except that ل has no cross bar and has a narrower and deeper tail that dips below the line in its independent and final positions. Note how similar the shapes of medial ل (alif) and ـلـ appear: the only difference is that ـلـ connects, while alif does not.

To write independent ل, start at the top and draw straight down, continuing below the line into the tail, which should be approximately the same shape as the tail of س , but a little narrower. **The tail must come all the way back up above the line.** Copy the example as shown:

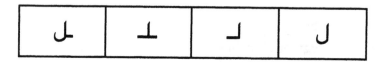

Initial ـل is begun the same way, down to the line. Rather than drawing the tail, continue into the connecting segment along the line. Write initial ـل in ليبيا :

To write medial ⊥, start from the connecting segment, draw up and then trace back down to the line into the next connecting segment as shown. Practice ⊥ by copying بَلَد (*country*):

When writing ل followed by ج , ح , or خ , the shape of ل is somewhat shorter because it goes into the connecting segment for these letters before it reaches the line. Practice writing this shape in the following words:

(*she insists*) تُلِحّ   (*dates*) بَلَح   (*woman's name*) صالحة   (*snow*) ثَلج

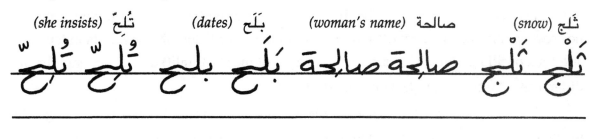

To write final ل, drop the connecting segment and draw a big rounded tail. Be sure to dip well below the line and finish the hook by bringing the pen all the way back up to the line again. Practice by writing طَويل (*long*):

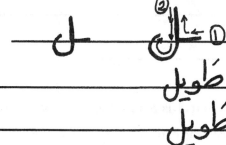

لا

laam alif

The distinct shape of the combination of ل + ا (laam followed by alif) is not part of the Arabic alphabet, but must be used to join these letters wherever they occur in this order in the same word. This shape varies slightly in print and handwriting styles. The form you see in the box above is the one you will see in print. Some people write it this way by hand as well, in one stroke:

In most handwriting styles, however, لا is written in two separate strokes, as Ustaaz El-Shinnawi does on your DVD. To produce this handwritten form, start as you would connected ل , but instead of drawing the body straight down, curve it to the left just above the line. When you reach the line, pick up your pen and make a slanted alif stroke into the corner of ل as the example shows. Write the word لا *no*:

Remember that the alif does not connect to a following letter, therefore, لا **does not connect** to anything following it. Copy and pronounce the following words:

أولاد (*children*)   كلاب (*dogs*)   بِلاد (*countries*)   صَلاة (*prayer*)

DRILL 8. DVD
DICTATION.

1. _____   6. _____

2. _____   7. _____

3. _____   8. _____

4. _____   9. _____

5. _____   10. _____

DRILL 9. DVD
YOU WILL HEAR TEN WORDS. CIRCLE THE WORD YOU HEAR IN EACH ROW:

1.	كَلَب	قَلَب	كِلاب	قَلْب
2.	أضلّ	أظلّ	أطلّ	أذلّ
3.	عاقِل	عِقال	أكل	عَقل
4.	فِقرة	فكَّر	فِكَر	فَقر
5.	تكلّ	شكَل	ثكَل	صَقَل
6.	ركَل	رفَس	ركَض	رقَص
7.	شرَف	ظرَف	صرَف	ذرَف
8.	تَقرير	تكرير	تكدير	تَقدير
9.	خِزي	حوذي	خُذي	حُزّي
10.	بلَج	بلَع	بلَح	بلَغ

DRILL 10. DVD
FILL IN THE CONSONANT THAT YOU HEAR IN EACH OF THE FOLLOWING :

1.	تَـ ـ قيد	8.	صـ ـ ير
2.	ـ رُفـة	9.	ـ ديق
3.	ـ يْـف	10.	شَخْـ ـ يّة
4.	فُـ ـ ور	11.	ـ ريف
5.	ـ قارِب	12.	ـ حِكَت
6.	تَـ ـ ليل	13.	تَـ ـ بُل
7.	ـ ابِق	14.	ـ جر

- 98 -

DRILL 11. 📀
DICTATION.

1. _____   6. _____
2. _____   7. _____
3. _____   8. _____
4. _____   9. _____
5. _____   10. _____

ARABIC SIGNS 📀
READ THE ARABIC SIGNS ON DVD WITH YOUR TEACHER. SOUND OUT THE WORDS AND NAMES. WHICH ONES DO YOU RECOGNIZE?

VOCABULARY 📀
GO TO YOUR DVD TO LISTEN TO AND LEARN THESE NOUNS (THEY INCLUDE *CHAIR, TABLE, STORY, SHEET OF PAPER, CLASS, SUGAR, NOTEBOOK, PAGE, ROOM, MILK, BOOK, MONEY* AND *WINDOW*).

صَفحة   شُبّاك   سُكَّر   دَفتَر   حَليب

فُلـوس   فَصل/صَفّ   غُرفة   طاولة   طالب/ة

وَرَقة   كِتاب   كُرسي   قصَّة

YOU WILL ALSO SEE AND HEAR THESE ADJECTIVES; GUESS THEIR MEANING FROM THE PICTURES (THEY INCLUDE *NEAR, FAR, TALL, SHORT, LARGE, SMALL* AND *NICE*):

كَبيرة/ة   قَصيرة/ة   طَويل/ة   قَريب/ة   بَعيد/ة

لَطيف/ة   صَغيرة/ة

LEARN:

GOOD, FINE   كُوَيِّس/ة

DRILL 12.
MATCH THE WORDS YOU LEARNED WITH THESE PICTURES, AND DESCRIBE THEM USING ADJECTIVES.

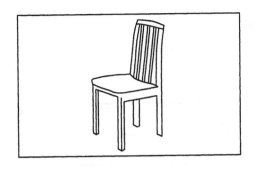

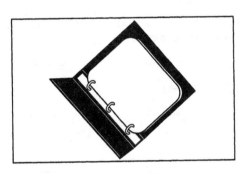
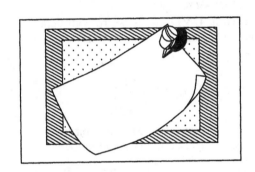

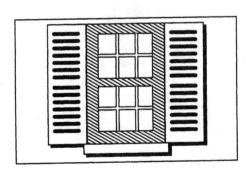
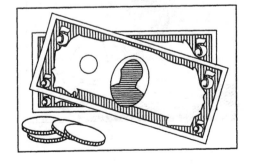

DIALOGUES 📀

CULTURE: اِتفَضَّلي / اِتفَضَّل 📀

Just as greeting people when you first see them is essential to courteous behavior taking leave is also expected. Whether sitting at a meal or just standing around chatting, you must excuse yourself before leaving. People usually say:

عَن إذنَك / عَن إذنِك ‏ *ᶜan iznak* / *ᶜan iznik*[1]

which means *with your permission*, and the usual response is:

اِتفَضَّل / اِتفَضَّلي

which means *please, go ahead*. You have also heard *itfaDDal/i* used to mean *please, come in / sit down*, and it can also mean *please, help yourself* (for example, to food).

Watch the scenes on your DVD that show various uses of اتفضّل / اتفضّلي and determine the context and meaning of this expression in each case. Practice by acting out similar scenes with your classmates.

---

[1]Remember that in Cairo, Beirut, and Damascus, ذ is often pronounced *z*.

هـ   ن   م

In this unit, you will learn the last three letters of the alphabet, the numbers 1-10, and more vocabulary.

م

miim

This letter corresponds to English *m* as in *may*.

LISTENING EXERCISE 1. DVD

LISTEN TO THE WORDS CONTAINING م AND REPEAT.

كلام   يوم   جامعة   مصر   سمير   مال

WRITING DVD

ـم	ـمـ	مـ	م

م is a connecting letter whose basic shape is easily identifiable: a small, round loop. You can see from the words above that the printed forms do not vary much; however, the way the loop is drawn and connected to other letters varies in handwriting. It is important that you watch Ustaaz El-Shinnawi draw these shapes and practice the direction of the loop in each position until you can write it easily, without having to stop and check.

To write independent م , begin on the line and draw a small, round loop over and around to the right, continue along the line a short distance, then make a corner and draw the tail straight down, well below the line. Copy:

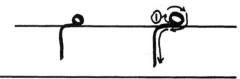

Practice by copying the word اليوم *today*:

اليوم اليوم

_____

There are two common styles of writing initial ﻤ . It may be looped up and over, just like independent م , or looped from underneath, in the opposite direction. Once you have closed the loop, continue on into a connecting segment. Copy and practice both examples, then choose one form to use:

_____

Now write the Arabic name for Egypt, مِصر :

مصر مصر

_____

When writing initial ﻤ followed by ج , ح , or خ , remember to draw the loop well above the line so that you can continue directly into the next letter. Copy the name مَجيد :

مجيد مجيد

_____

Medial ـمـ should **always loop down** from the connecting segment, which rests slightly above the line as the example shows. Watch Ustaaz El-Shinnawi and copy:

Copy these names containing combinations of ـمـ and ج /ح/خ :

حميدة   محمد   جميلة   خميس

حميدة حميدة   محمد محمد   جميلة جميلة   خميس خميس

In some typefaces and handwriting styles, ـمـ may be joined to **initial** letters ـب , ـت , ـث , ـيـ , and ـ as shown: بم , تم , يم , and م . Below are both print and handwritten examples of common words. Copy, making sure to loop medial and final م **downward**:

(fine) تمام   *(with what?)* بم   *(boring)* ممل   *(excellent)* ممتاز

ممتاز ممتاز   ممل ممل   بم , بم ,   تمام تمام تمام

When م follows an unconnected ل , it is usually written in the corner formed when ل meets the line as shown. Copy the example:

Be on the lookout for this ـلـ combination, especially in print, where ـم often appears as a little bump on the right of ـل . Copy and sound out:

(when) لَمَّا   (Mexico) اَلْمَكْسيك   (diamonds) ألْماس   (Morocco) اَلْمَغْرِب

لمَّا لمَّا المكـسيك المكـسيك ألماس ألماس المغرب المغرب

In handwriting, final ـم must be looped **down** from the top. Starting from the connecting segment, continue into the loop, then circle down and around to the right, making a full loop, then continue into the tail. Watch Ustaaz El-Shinnawi on the DVD, follow the arrows, and practice:

Read and copy these names ending in ـم :   (ميم جيم كَريم حَليم سالِم)

Copy and read aloud the following names (first line female; second, male):

كَريمة   مَيّ   جَميلة   ماجِدة   أمَل

عِصام عِمـاد   حامد   أحمَد   سامِر

Drill 1.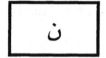
Dictation.

1. _____   5. _____

2. _____   6. _____

3. _____   7. _____

4. _____   8. _____

ن

nuun

This letter represents the sound *n* as in *noon*.

Listening Exercise 2.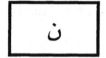

LISTEN AND READ ALOUD WORDS CONTAINING ن .

سَنـة   غَنِيّ   إيران   تونِس   لُبنـان   نار

Writing

ـن	ـنـ	نـ	ن

ن is a connecting letter whose shape resembles that of ب in initial and medial positions, except for the placement of the dot. It differs from ب in that the independent and final forms of ن take a characteristic "tail" shape that dips well below the line. Watch the DVD and practice drawing the shape of independent ن , making sure to **bring the tail back up across the line:**

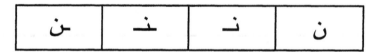

At the beginning or in the middle of a word, write ـنـ as you write ب , but dot above rather than below the letter. Copy:

Read aloud and copy:

عِندي (I have)   تـونِس   نَبي (prophet)

_____

_____

In final position, ــن begins with a tooth and then dips immediately into a deep tail below the line. Bring the tail back up **across the line**. Practice final ن by copying these names:

أَيْـمَن (male)   مَيان (female)   لُبْـنان   نـون

_____

_____

Read aloud and copy the following names (top line female, bottom line male):

أماني   حَـنان   نَجاة   نَفيسة   إيمان   زَيْـنَب

_____

_____

رَمَضان   عَدنان   مُنـذِر   جُبـران   ناجي   أمـين

_____

_____

DRILL 2.

READ ALOUD THESE NAMES OF COUNTRIES AND CITIES:

باريـس	فَرَنْـسا	بَـنغلاديش	قَـطَـر
أَلْـمانـيا	بَلجيكا	نيويورك	بَغْداد
إفْريـقيا	موسكو	كولـومبيـا	كَنَدا
طَـرابُـلُس	أمْريـكا	أوسْتراليا	لُنـدُن
باكِستان	بَيـروت	أفْغانِسْتان	سوريا
بريـطانـيا	صَنْعاء	موريتانـيا	عَمّـان

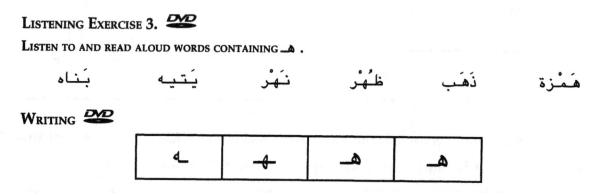

DRILL 3.
DICTATION.

1. _____   6. _____

2. _____   7. _____

3. _____   8. _____

4. _____   9. _____

5. _____   10. _____

```
ـه
```

haa

This letter represents a familiar sound, the one spelled in English by *h* as in *house*. Unlike English *h*, which can be silent, as in *hour* , ـه is always pronounced. Moreover, the English *h* sound tends to occur at the beginning of a word or syllable, whereas Arabic ـه can occur in any position. Say *a house* , then say the two words as if they were a single word. This is how ـه sounds in the middle of a word. Now say *her*, then say it backwards, pronouncing the *h*. This is how ـه sounds at the end of a word.

LISTENING EXERCISE 3.

LISTEN TO AND READ ALOUD WORDS CONTAINING ـه .

بَنــاه   يَتيــه   نَهْر   ظـُهْر   ذَهَب   هَمْـزة

WRITING

ـه	ـهـ	ـهـ	ه

The forms of this connecting letter vary more than those of any other. In addition, individual style can affect its shape in initial and medial forms. Watch Ustaaz El-Shinnawi on the DVD and copy his handwriting. The shape ـه is the form this letter takes independently and at the beginning of a word. To write this shape, begin slightly above the line, and draw a large loop sloping first upward and then downward to your right and back up. This outer loop should be large; its exact shape can vary according to individual style and print type from a more pointed to a more rounded oval. When you reach the beginning of the loop,

continue on, making a small loop inside the big one, then continue on down to the line into the connecting segment. Copy the example:

Copy the name of the consonant همزة :

In medial position, ـه has two main variations. The first is more common in print: ـهـ (look also at the printed form of the words in Listening Exercise 3 above); it consists of two vertical loops, one above and one below the line. The second is more commonly found in handwriting and is written in one stroke as a (more or less) pointed dip below the line. Copy the example:

Copy and sound out the female name مَها :

Final ـه takes the same connected and unconnected shapes as ـة (تاء مربوطة), **except that it has no dots. It is important to distinguish between these two letters: while ـة is** generally a feminine marker, ـه often indicates the possessive *his/its*. To write unconnected final ه , simply start above the line and draw a fat oval, just as you drew ة :

To write final ـه connected with a previous letter, start from the connecting segment and draw a short line up, then loop around into a flat oval. The exact shape of this oval varies according to individual style and print type. Copy:

The letter ـه occurs regularly at the end of words because it represents the possessive pronoun *his/its*. To practice writing final ه and ـه, copy and sound out:

اِسمُهُ   دَفترُهُ   أُستاذُهُ   بَيتُهُ

Now copy and sound out the following names (top line female, bottom line male):

زَهْرة   سُهَيْر   سُهَيْلة   هِيام   هَناء

بَهاء   سُهَيْل   هاني   فَهْد   هَيْثَم

DRILL 4. 📀

LISTEN TO THE WORDS ON TAPE, DECIDE WHETHER THE FINAL LETTER YOU HEAR IS ة OR ه , AND WRITE IT IN THE BLANK. ALSO WRITE IN ALL THE SHORT VOWELS THAT YOU HEAR:

1. أبا ـــ ــــ   3. مدينـ ـــ ــــ   5. دراسـ ـــ ــــ   7. في بيتـ ـــ ــــ

2. ميا ـــ ــــ   4. كتبـ ـــ ــــ   6. دكتورا ـــ ــــ   8. جميـل ـــ ــــ

Remember that ه is different from ح . ه is a sound that exists in English and is very easy for English speakers to pronounce, whereas ح is pronounced deep in the throat and has a slightly raspy sound. You can say ه without thinking about your throat muscles, but you must concentrate to say ح . It is important to distinguish between these two sounds, so go back to the alphabet chart to watch and listen. The following exercises will also help.

LISTENING EXERCISE 4. 📀

LISTEN TO THE CONTRAST BETWEEN ه AND ح IN THE FOLLOWING PAIRS OF WORDS:

هَـمْـزة / حَـمْـزة	هَـل / حَـل	هُـبـوب / حُـبـوب	نَـهْـر / نَـحْـر
بَـلَـه / بَـلَـح	فَـهْـم / فَـحْـم	أبْـهَـر / أبْـحَـر	نَـهَـل / نَـحَـل

DRILL 5. 📀

YOU WILL HEAR TWELVE WORDS . FOR EACH, CIRCLE THE SOUND YOU HEAR:

1. ه ح		5. ه ح		9. ه ح	
2. ه ح		6. ه ح		10. ه ح	
3. ه ح		7. ه ح		11. ه ح	
4. ه ح		8. ه ح		12. ه ح	

DRILL 6. 📀

READ THE FOLLOWING ALOUD WITH THE DVD, PAYING PARTICULAR ATTENTION TO ح AND ه :

1. (a) حَوْل	(b) هَوْل		7. (a) أحرَقَ	(b) أهرَقَ
2. (a) حَمَد	(b) هَمَد		8. (a) مُبحِر	(b) مُبهِر
3. (a) شَحْم	(b) شَهْم		9. (a) ناحِية	(b) ناهِية
4. (a) جُحود	(b) جُهود		10. (a) اِستِحلال	(b) اِستِهلال
5. (a) حافي	(b) هافي		11. (a) إحفام	(b) إفهام
6. (a) طَحَل	(b) طَهَل		12. (a) أصحَرَ	(b) أصهَرَ

DRILL 7. 📀

WRITE THE LETTER THAT YOU HEAR IN EACH BLANK:

1. رَ ___ بة	4. ضا ___ ك	7. ___ رِ ___ يّة	10. ___ ثالة
2. فَ ___ يَم	5. لِ ___ اف	8. صَ ___ راء	11. مشـ ___ ور
3. جَبَ ___ ات	6. ظُ ___ ور	9. أ ___ م	12. ___ مّام

1. _____   3. _____   5. _____

2. _____   4. _____   6. _____

DRILL 9.

THE FOLLOWING IS A TYPICAL NEWSPAPER WORD GAME TAKEN FROM THE DAILY "AL-SHARQ AL-AWSAT." IN THE BOX BELOW, LOOK FOR THE WORDS LISTED IN THE TWO COLUMNS TO THE RIGHT, RUNNING IN ANY DIRECTION. ONCE YOU FIND THE WORD, CIRCLE IT OR DRAW A LINE THROUGH IT. AFTER YOU HAVE FOUND ALL THE WORDS, WRITE OUT THE REMAINING UNUSED LETTERS. THEY WILL SPELL THE NAME OF A FAMOUS BIBLICAL/QURANIC PROPHET.

الكلمة الضائعة

ج	ن	ق	ص	ا	ن	م	ع	د
ف	س	ج	ف	ر	ش	ي	ع	ا
ا	ع	و	و	س	ح	ص	ا	ن
ف	ي	ف	ا	ا	ف	ي	ن	ز
ك	د	م	ج	و	ع	ا	ب	س
ع	ح	ة	ر	ق	ي	ب	و	ب
ك	ظ	ي	غ	ز	و	س	ب	ك
ض	ع	ي	ف	ر	ن	ة	ف	و
ز	ي	ا	د	ة	ن	أ	ش	ك

عصفور	زيادة
عيون	يابسة
انبوب	ضعيف
زناد	سامح
رزق	كعك
كوكب	حاجة
جوف	نقصان
جفاف	غيظ
شرف	شأن
عم	سعيد

من جريدة الشرق الاوسط ، ١٩٩٢

LISTENING EXERCISE 5. 📀 THE COMPLETE ALPHABET

مـا شـاء الله! YOU HAVE LEARNED TO WRITE AND PRONOUNCE ALL THE LETTERS OF THE ARABIC ALPHABET. THIS CHART PRESENTS THE NAMES AND ORDER OF THE LETTERS. YOU MUST LEARN THIS ORDER TO BE ABLE TO USE A DICTIONARY. BEGIN BY LISTENING TO THE DVD.

ث	ت	ب	ا
ثاء	تاء	باء	ألف
د	خ	ح	ج
دال	خاء	حاء	جيم
س	ز	ر	ذ
سين	زاي	راء	ذال
ط	ض	ص	ش
طاء	ضاد	صاد	شين
ف	غ	ع	ظ
فاء	غَين	عَين	ظاء
م	ل	ك	ق
ميم	لام	كاف	قاف
ي	و	هـ	ن
ياء	واو	هاء	نون

LISTENING EXERCISE 6. 📀
SURPRISE! LISTEN TO THE DVD.

- 114 -

DRILL 10.
LISTED BELOW ARE NAMES OF SOME ARAB AUTHORS YOU NEED TO INCLUDE IN A BIBLIOGRAPHY. ALPHABETIZE THEM ACCORDING TO THE ARABIC ALPHABET, BUT DISREGARD الـ .

مُطران	عَوَض	بساط	الخوري	الكَيّالي
صَفيّ الدّين	نادِر	الشَّيْخ	وَهبَه	السَّنهوري
الخَليل	مُهَنّا	صابِر	جَفّال	العِنداري
غُرَيِّب	زايد	القاسِم	الغانِم	الخالِدي
عَبد الرّازِق	السَّمّان	القَبّاني	دَرويش	الدُّسوقي

ARABIC NUMERALS AND NUMBERS

LISTENING EXERCISE 7. *DVD*
LISTEN TO THE DVD AND LEARN THE ARABIC NAMES FOR THESE NUMERALS:

Two related sets of numerals, shown in the chart, are used in the Arab world. The set in the right column developed in the Maghreb (Morocco, Algeria, and Tunisia) and is used increasingly in print news media, while the one in the middle column evolved and remains common in the Arab east. The numerals used in the Arab west were introduced into Europe from Islamic Spain in the Middle Ages—hence our name for them, Arabic numerals. Arab and Muslim mathematicians adopted their numerals from India, and expanded on earlier Hindu and Greek contributions to develop algebra and other branches of higher mathematics.

صِفر	٠	0
واحِد	١	1
اِثنان/اِثنَين	٢	2
ثَلاثة	٣	3
أربَعة	٤	4
خَمسة	٥	5
سِتّة	٦	6
سَبعة	٧	7
ثَمانية	٨	8
تِسعة	٩	9
عَشَرة	١٠	10

WRITING NUMERALS 1-10 📀

Most Arabic numerals appear in handwriting much the same way they appear in print, with the exception of ٢ and ٣. In print, they appear as shown above. In handwriting, however, they take on slightly different forms. Copy these examples:

You can see that the numeral ٢ in print closely resembles the numeral ٣ when written by hand, except that the hook at the top of handwritten ٣ is usually deeper. To avoid confusion, always write these numerals as shown in the handwritten example above, and when reading, remember to differentiate between printed and handwritten forms. Now watch Ustaaz El-Shinnawi write the numbers 1-10 and copy the examples. Note that zero is written as a dot:

١٠   ٩   ٨   ٧   ٦   ٥   ٤   ٣   ٢   ١

WRITING NUMBERS GREATER THAN 9

Arabic numbers are not written from right to left but rather from left to right, just like numbers in English. The reason for this is that Arabic numbers were traditionally **read** from right to left in the same direction they are written: ones, then tens, then hundreds, and so on. Only recently have larger numbers (hundreds and above) came to be read before ones and tens.

Compare the following English and Arabic equivalents of various numbers. Note that Arabic uses a comma rather than a period for the decimal point, and does not normally mark commas in large numbers or hyphens in telephone numbers:

٢٫٥٠	١٠٧٨٩	٥٦٩٠٨٩٤	١٩٥٥	٣٢٥
2.50	10,789	569-0894	1955	325

Now practice writing large numbers by writing out your telephone number and the year of your birth:

DRILL 11.

PREPARE FOR THIS ACTIVITY BY MEMORIZING YOUR TELEPHONE NUMBER IN ARABIC NUMERALS. IN CLASS, GET THE NAMES AND PHONE NUMBERS OF YOUR CLASSMATES — IN ARABIC! — AND WRITE THEM BELOW:

Address العُنـوان	Telephone No. رَقم التليفون	Name الاسـم

ARABIC SIGNS DVD

READ THE ARABIC SIGNS ON DVD WITH YOUR TEACHER. SOUND OUT THE WORDS AND NAMES. WHICH ONES DO YOU RECOGNIZE?

VOCABULARY 📀

Go to your DVD to listen to and learn these words (they include *TEST, PEN/PENCIL, GIRL, BOY, LIBRARY, OFFICE, WORD, WATER, COFFEE, WOMAN, MAN, BUILDING,* and *BEAUTIFUL*):

كلمة   مَكتَبة   مَكتَب   قَلَم   بِناية

بنت   ولد   امرأة   رجل   *DRILL* تَمرين

ماء   قهوة أمريكية   قهوة عربية   جميل/ة   اِمْتِحان

DRILL 12.

Match the words you learned with these pictures, and write a phrase or sentence about each one.

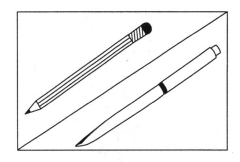

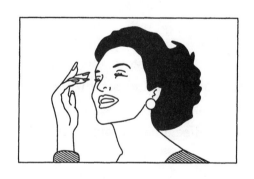

DIALOGUES 📀

WATCH SCENE 9 YALLA! يلا! WITH YOUR TEACHER.

CULTURE: COFFEE TIME!

MAKING COFFEE 📀

by Michael Cooperson

Coffee and tea are the most popular social drinks in the Arab world. They are served to visitors at home and in the workplace, and men gather to drink them in coffeehouses. Some coffeehouses in upscale areas are also becoming popular among women. The choice between coffee and tea is partly a matter of local custom and supply, and partly a matter of personal taste. In much of North Africa, tea is more common, and is often made with loose green tea and mint, and drunk very sweet. In restaurants, coffee is usually served European style.

In Egypt and the Levant, Arabic coffee (also called Turkish coffee) is a strong drink made from very finely ground, dark beans, boiled in a little pot, and often served in demitasse cups or glasses. Watch your DVD to see how it is made. In Egypt, unless you request otherwise, coffee will be served to you *maZbuuT*, which means *just right*, referring to the amount of sugar (about one teaspoon per small cup). Tea is also popular, and served sweet.

In the Arabian Peninsula, another kind of Arabic coffee is served. The coffee beans are roasted in a different manner, and the coffee itself is almost clear in color and has a unique flavor. It is served in tiny cups without handles, and the cup is refilled by the host until the guest signals that he or she has had enough by tilting it from side to side several times.

AT THE COFFEEHOUSE 📀

Coffeehouses are popular meeting places, although by custom, they are frequented more by men than women in most Arab countries (women tend to socialize in houses for privacy). In addition to coffee, tea, and other hot drinks, games such as chess and backgammon are available. Watch scenes from some traditional coffeehouses around Cairo on your DVD.

الوحدة الثامنة

UNIT EIGHT

In this unit, you will learn about the definite article, more about initial hamza, an old spelling for alif that still survives in a few words, and more vocabulary.

الـ

أَلِف لام

Called in Arabic أَلِف لام after the names of the letters, the segment الـ represents the definite article in Arabic, similar to *the* in English. Compare these two pairs of nouns:

كتاب *a book*   الكتاب *the book*   أستاذ *a teacher*   الأستاذ *the teacher*

These examples show that الـ makes an indefinite noun definite. Of course, the usage of Arabic الـ is not exactly equivalent to that of English *the*. For example, you have already learned how to say:

جامعة القاهرة   *The University of Cairo*

in which جامعة is definite although it does not have الـ. You will learn more about the usage of الـ over the next few weeks; in the meantime, remember that **a word modified by الـ is definite**.

Proper nouns are definite whether or not they begin with الـ; for example, مصر *Egypt* is definite, as is القاهرة. Foreign (non-Arabic) names, such as the names of European countries and cities, generally do not take الـ. The names of Arab cities and countries must be memorized, because there is no rule that determines whether or not they take الـ.

LISTENING EXERCISE 1. 📀

LISTEN TO THESE WORDS WITH AND WITHOUT الـ.

بيت – البيت   قلم – القلم   مكتب – المكتب

أستاذة – الاستاذة   مكتبة – المكتبة   كرسي – الكرسي

PRONUNCIATION OF الـ

الـ has a special pronunciation rule which dictates that, before certain letters, لـ is not pronounced as لـ , but is elided to or "swallowed by" the following consonant. As a result, the following consonant takes a shadda and is pronounced as a doubled consonant because it has "swallowed" the sound of the لـ while retaining its length. For example, the word الدكتور is pronounced *ad-duktuur* (**not** *al-duktuur*) because د is one of the letters that assimilates the لـ of الـ . The letters that assimilate this لـ are called الحُروف الشَّـمـسيّة (*sun letters*, pronounced *al-Huruuf ash-shamsiyya*), after the word شَـمـس (*sun*), which begins with ش , one of the letters that assimilates لـ . The consonants that do not assimilate the لـ are called الحُروف القَمَرية (*moon letters*, pronounced *al-Huruuf al-qamariyya*), because the ق of قَمَر (*moon*) is one of the letters that do not assimilate لـ .

LISTENING EXERCISE 2. 📀

LISTEN TO THESE WORDS WITH SUN AND MOON LETTERS AND REPEAT, WITH SPECIAL ATTENTION TO THE PRONUNCIATION OF الـ :

الأوتوبيس	الكتاب	الاستاذ	القلم	البيت	الحروف القمرية:
الطّائرة	الطّاولة	الصّفّ	السّيّارة	الشّارع	الحروف الشـمسية:

Note that the first group of words contains the sound لـ , whereas in the second, you do not hear لـ , but rather a shadda on the following consonant. This shadda is sometimes written in, as it is above, as a reminder of correct pronunciation. In fully vocalized texts, it is considered part of proper vowelling, and will always be written in. It is a good idea to write the shadda on الحـروف الشـمسـية for now, until you have memorized them and remember to read الـ correctly.

The following chart lists the letters in their proper classes. As a rule of thumb, note that الحـروف الشـمسـية —the letters that swallow the لـ —are the ones whose tongue position is close to that of لـ . This rule will help you **memorize** which group each letter belongs to so that you can speak and read Arabic correctly:

الـ + الحُروف الشَمسيّة والحُروف القَمَريّة	
ت ث د ذ ر ز س ش ص ض ط ظ ل ن	الحروف الشـمسية
أ ب ج ح خ ع غ ف ق ك م هـ و ي	الحروف القمرية

DRILL 1. 📀

MAKE THESE INDEFINITE WORDS DEFINITE BY ADDING الــ, AND WRITE شــدّة ON THE WORDS THAT BEGIN

WITH حروف شمسية, THEN READ ALOUD:

٨ـ سلام	————	١ـ جامعة	————
٩ـ مدينة	————	٢ـ اسم	————
١٠ـ أستاذة	————	٣ـ طالب	————
١١ـ كتاب	————	٤ـ شريط	————
١٢ـ صباح	————	٥ـ فصل	————
١٣ـ درس	————	٦ـ قهوة	————
١٤ـ باب	————	٧ـ ورقة	————

DRILL 2. 📀

WRITE شدّة ON THE حروف شمسية IN THE FOLLOWING WORDS, AND WRITE سكون ON THE لـ BEFORE

حروف قمرية, AS IN THE EXAMPLES. THEN READ THE WORDS ALOUD.

Examples: الْقَلَم   الـرّاديـو

الشارع	الطائرة	الـمدينة	البيْت	الدكتور
السيارة	القرآن	الديمُقراطي	الصـف	الكَعبة
النَهـر	السؤال	الغَزال	العَيْن	اللَوح
الثَقافة	الخَير	الحِزب	الإسلام	الظَلام

DRILL 3. 📀

CIRCLE THE WORD YOU HEAR IN EACH ROW. PAY SPECIAL ATTENTION TO THE FIRST SYLLABLE IN EACH WORD
AND LISTEN FOR THE PRESENCE OR ABSENCE OF SHADDA ON SUN LETTERS.

صوم	أصوم	الصوم	٦ـ	أسلم	إسلام	السلام	١ـ
أصبح	الصباح	صباح	٧ـ	صفّ	الصفّ	أصفّ	٢ـ
الظلام	أظلم	ظلام	٨ـ	أعمل	عمل	العمل	٣ـ
ثاني	أثاني	الثاني	٩ـ	أنهاية	نهاية	النهاية	٤ـ
نور	النور	أنور	١٠ـ	أقلام	قلم	القلم	٥ـ

DRILL 4. DVD

YOU WILL HEAR TWELVE WORDS. WRITE ال FOR EACH WORD THAT CONTAINS IT AND Ø FOR EACH WORD THAT DOES NOT.

١._____   ٧_____   ٤._____   ١-_____

١١-_____   ٨_____   ٥._____   ٢-_____

١٢-_____   ٩_____   ٦-_____   ٣-_____

DRILL 5. DVD

YOU WILL HEAR EIGHT PHRASES. DETERMINE WHETHER THE SECOND WORD IN EACH IS DEFINITE OR INDEFINITE, AND WRITE ال FOR THOSE THAT ARE DEFINITE AND Ø FOR THOSE THAT ARE INDEFINITE:

٧-_____   ٥-_____   ٣-_____   ١-_____

٨-_____   ٦-_____   ٤-_____   ٢-_____

DRILL 6.

READ ALOUD THE FOLLOWING WORDS WITH ATTENTION TO ال AND حروف شمسية :

الزِّيارة	الخاصّ	اللَّيلة	الطّالِب	البَحْرَين
الوَلَد	الدّار	النّيل	الإمارات	الكُوَيت
المَغرِب	الفارّ	الحَليب	الأُردُن	الضّباب
الشّبّاك	الثّاني	الدَّوحة	السّودان	الخَرْطوم
الرِّباط	اليَمَن	الذّهاب	الظّلام	الغالي
الصّومال	العِراق	القلم	التّونِسي	الجَزائِر

DRILL 7. DVD

DICTATION. REMEMBER THAT YOU WILL NOT HEAR ل IN ال ON WORDS THAT BEGIN WITH حروف شمسية — LISTEN FOR SHADDA!

٩-_____   ٥-_____   ١-_____

١٠-_____   ٦-_____   ٢-_____

١١-_____   ٧-_____   ٣-_____

١٢-_____   ٨-_____   ٤-_____

هَمْزة الوَصْل

You have seen that words like أُستاذ begin with the consonant هَمْزة (whether or not it is written: ا or أ). It is the هَمْزة that "allows" you to pronounce the vowel that follows it. In most words that begin with هَمْزة , the vowel that the hamza carries always remains the same; for example, أُستاذ is always pronounced the same way, with a ضَمّة . However, the هَمْزة of الـ belongs to a special category called هَمْزة الوَصْل , which means *elidable hamza*. "Elidable" means that, when preceded by another word, the hamza and its vowel drop in both pronunciation and writing. In writing, the symbol *waSla* وَصلة takes the place of the هَمْزة , and in pronunciation, the original vowel on the alif is swallowed by the final vowel of a previous word or by a helping vowel. Thus, in the case of الـ , the normal فَتحة vowel on the alif is not usually heard.

LISTENING EXERCISE 3. *DVD*

LISTEN CAREFULLY TO الـ **IN THE SECOND WORD OF EACH PHRASE. YOU WILL NOT HEAR THE** ا **OF THE** الـ **BECAUSE IT IS SWALLOWED BY THE FINAL VOWEL OF THE PRECEDING WORD:**

في ٱلجامعة	في ٱلبيت	أمريكا ٱللاتينية	أبي ٱلعزيز
كرسي ٱلطالب	والدا ٱلبنت	مدرّسو ٱلجامعة	بيتي ٱلجديد

WRITING *DVD*

The symbol for هَمْزة الوَصْل , called وَصلة , is not normally written except in completely vowelled texts. It can only occur at the beginning of a word, and the overwhelming majority of cases occur on الـ . Practice writing it by copying the example:

ٱلـ ٱلـ ٱلـ

DRILL 8. 📀

LISTEN AS THE FOLLOWING PHRASES ARE READ ALOUD. SOME WILL CONTAIN REGULAR همـزة AND SOME WILL CONTAIN همزة الوصل. MARK EITHER وصلة OR همزة ACCORDING TO WHAT YOU HEAR:

٦ـ أينَ البيت ؟		١ـ	ما اسمك ؟	
٧ـ هُوَ احمد		٢ـ	والدي استاذ	
٨ـ في المدينة		٣ـ	عندي الم	
٩ـ أخو البنت		٤ـ	لي اسنان	
١٠ـ أنا الاستاذ		٥ـ	صديقي الفرنسي	

DRILL 9.

USE THE PREPOSITIONS TO FIGURE OUT THE MEANING OF THE FOLLOWING PHRASES, THEN READ THEM ALOUD, PAYING SPECIAL ATTENTION TO همـزة الوصل AND الحروف الشمسية والقمرية:

مِن from	مَعَ with	مِن in, at في
مِنَ المكتبة	مع الخُبز	من القاهرة	في الشاي
في الفصل	في الجامعة	من الشبّاك	في الشارع
مِنَ الكتاب	مَعَ القهوة	في البناية	في البيت
	في السيارة	في الأوتوبيس	من البيت

NOW CHOOSE SEVEN OF THESE PHRASES AND EXPAND THEM TO FORM SENTENCES SUCH AS:

الرّجل في الأوتوبيس.   الكتاب من المكتبة.

١ـ _____.

٢ـ _____.

٣ـ _____.

٤ـ _____.

٥ـ _____.

٦ـ _____.

٧ـ _____.

dagger alif

This symbol is often called *dagger alif* because its shape resembles a small dagger. It represents an old spelling of alif from early Qur'anic writing that survives today in a few common words and names. It is pronounced exactly like the long vowel alif.

LISTENING EXERCISE 4. DVD
LISTEN TO THESE WORDS CONTAINING DAGGER ALIF AND REPEAT:

عَبْد الرَحمٰـن   الله   لٰـكِـن   هٰـذا

LEARN THE FOLLOWING WORDS:

but	لٰـكِـن	*this* (masculine)	هٰـذا
God	الله	*this* (feminine)	هٰـذِه

These are most of the commonly used words that are spelled with dagger alif. It is almost never written, except in fully vowelled texts, but is important to learn the words that are spelled with it and remember to **pronounce this as a long vowel equivalent to alif.**

WRITING

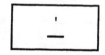

When dagger alif is written, it is drawn as a short vertical stroke above the consonant it follows. Make sure it is precisely vertical, so that it may be distinguished easily from the slanted fatHa. Copying the examples, practice writing and pronouncing the words you have just learned:

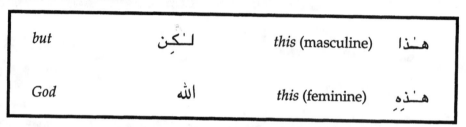

Drill 10.

Use the vocabulary you have learned so far to describe things with هذا and هذه . Remember to think about gender agreement.

This is a spacious room. هذه غرفة واسعة

This is good tea! هذا شاي طيّب !

Drill 11.

What is being advertised here? Skim through the following ad and look for words borrowed from English that you can sound out. Which words can you eliminate as being Arabic? (Hint: think of the emphatic letters that do not represent English sounds.)

من جريدة الشرق الاوسط ، ١٩٩٢

Arabic Signs DVD

Read the Arabic signs on DVD with your teacher and sound out the words and names.

Vocabulary DVD ازيّك؟

Before watching the DVD, study and learn these pronouns:

she هِيَ   *he* هُوَ   *you (fem.)* أنتِ   *you (masc.)* أنتَ   *I* أنا

NOW WATCH THE CARTOONS ON YOUR **DVD** AND LEARN THESE WORDS FROM CONTEXT (THEY INCLUDE *THIRSTY, HUNGRY, COLD, HOT, TIRED, EXHAUSTED, UPSET,* AND *SICK*):

بردان/ة	حرّان/ة	جوعان/ة	تعبان/ة
زَعلان/ة	خلصان/ة	مريض/ة	عطشان/ة

DRILL 12.
MATCH THE WORDS YOU LEARNED WITH THESE PICTURES, AND DESCRIBE THEM USING ADJECTIVES.

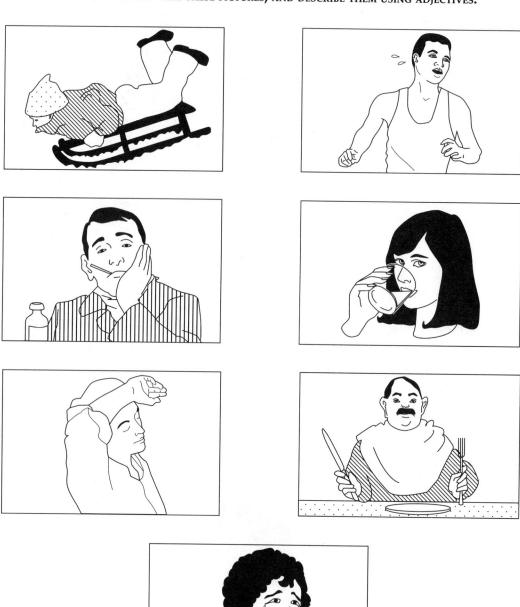

DIALOGUES 📀

WATCH SCENE 10 ألو AND SCENE 11 سَلامتَك! WITH YOUR TEACHER.

CULTURE

سَلامتَك!

The expression سَلامتَك (to a male) and سَلامتِك! (to a female) is roughly equivalent to *I hope you feel better!* or *Get well soon!* to someone who is ailing. If you are the one who is ailing, سَلامتَك!, and you should reply: الله يِسَلِّمَك (-ak to a male and -ik to a female).

سَلامتَك!!

«مَعْلِـهْش»

The colloquial expression «مَعلهش» (also spelled مَعليش) has a wide range of usages. It is used to say *never mind, don't worry about it, it doesn't matter,* in some cases, to say *is it okay (if I...)?,* and, finally, to console or calm someone who is upset or angry.

Some kinds of behavior that many Americans may see as interfering or speaking out of turn are quite acceptable in Arab culture. For example, when a person sees that someone is upset, he or she will probably try to find out what the problem is, and say معلهش—even if he or she does not know the person well.

معلهش!

الوحدة التاسعة
UNIT NINE

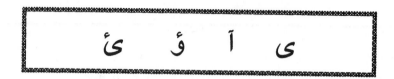

In this unit you will learn the final spelling of alif, which occurs only at the end of a word, and more about writing the consonant همزة .

أَلِف مَقصورة

Alif maqSuura, also called ألف بصورة الياء , *alif in the shape of yaa'*, is a variant spelling of alif that can only occur at the **end** of a word. This shape of alif is a spelling convention that dates back to the writing of the Qur'an. It is pronounced just like the regular alif. When the long vowel alif occurs at the end of a word, it is often spelled with alif maqSuura (for example, several prepositions and commonly used verbs contain this spelling). Foreign (non-Arabic) words and names are not usually spelled with alif maqSuura.

LISTENING EXERCISE 1. 📀

LISTEN TO THE FOLLOWING EXAMPLES OF WORDS ENDING IN أَلِف مقصورة **AND REPEAT:**

مُثَنَّى   اِنْتَهى   بَكى   مَشى   إلى   عَلى

WRITING 📀

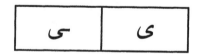

ى is a connector, and since it only occurs in final position, it has only the two shapes you see above. It is written exactly like final ي , **except that it has no dots.** In other words, final ي and ى are distinguished by the two dots of the ي , **except in Egypt, where both are usually written without dots.** Watch Ustaaz El-Shinnawi write this letter on your

DVD and copy the example:

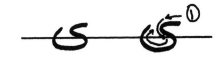

Copy and read aloud the following female names that end in ى :

نُهى   نَجوى   سَلـمى   مُنـى   لَيْلى

DRILL 1.

LEARN THE PREPOSITIONS إلى TO (AS IN GOING TO/MOTION TOWARDS) AND عَلى (ON TOP OF) AND COMPLETE:

A. NAME FIVE PLACES YOU GO TO EVERY DAY:

I go to   أذهَب إلى

EXAMPLE: أذهَب إلى الجامـعة

B. PLACE OBJECTS YOU CAN NAME ON TOP OF EACH OTHER AND DESCRIBE.

EXAMPLE: الكتاب على الطاولة

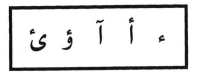

الـهـمـزة

MORE ABOUT HAMZA

Thus far, you have learned to write هـمـزة on an alif at the beginning of a word, and you have seen that it can be written by itself in the middle or at the end of a word. Here we present three other ways to write هـمـزة . At the beginning of the word, هـمـزة is always written on alif no matter what vowel sound follows it. Elsewhere, rules for the writing of هـمـزة depend on the vowels surrounding it.

أَلِف مَدَّة

What happens when هـمـزة is followed by the long vowel alif? The Arabic word *al-Qur'aan* is one word that contains the consonant هـمـزة followed by an alif. This combination can occur at the beginning or in the middle of a word, and in each case it is spelled in the same way, with a symbol that means "هـمـزة plus long vowel alif." This symbol, shown in the box above, is called *madda*, مَـدَّة , which means *lengthening*. It can only occur on alif, and when it does, the combination is called alif madda, أَلِف مَـدَّة . The alif madda represents the combination of **either ا + أ or ا + أ and is always pronounced as** هـمـزة followed by long vowel alif. These two combinations are never written separately, for the same historical reason that هـمـزة is written on different seats: when Arabic was first written, هـمـزة was not yet a part of the script. The symbols for هـمـزة and مَدّة were added to the alphabet later with the other extra-alphabetical markings. **Remember:** Like medial and final هـمـزة, the مَدّة sign must be written wherever it occurs.

LISTENING EXERCISE 2. DVD
LISTEN TO WORDS CONTAINING ALIF MADDA AND REPEAT:

مِرآة   الآن   القُرآن   آكُل   آمين   آن

WRITING DVD

أ

The مَدّة sign written above the الف is written as a slightly wavy line just above it. Copy the example:

Practice writing madda in القُرآن (the Quran) and الآن (now):

القُرآن

الآن

ؤ ، ئ

هَمزة على كُرسي الواو/الياء

When hamza occurs in the middle of a word, it may be written on top of alif, or rest on the line, **or** it may be written on a seat that has the shape of و or ي : ؤ or ئ . In this case, the و or ي does **not** function as a vowel, but serves as a seat, كرسي , for هَمزة .

The choice of seat for هَمزة is determined by the surrounding vowel sounds. When هَمزة occurs in the middle of a word, it may be preceded or followed by any of the vowel sounds, short or long. As you read the following sections, keep in mind the following hierarchy of vowel sounds: ي/كَسرة is the strongest vowel sound, followed by و/ضَمّة , and in last place, ١/فتحة . The general principle at work here is that هَمزة is written on the كرسي that matches the strongest vowel sound on either side of it.

ئ

همزة على كُرسي الياء

Whenever hamza in the middle of a word is **immediately preceded or followed by a كَسرة or long vowel ي** (i.e., when the vowel **on** the hamza is kasra), hamza is written on a ئ seat: ئ or ئـ . **Remember: when ى serves as a كرسي همزة , it takes no dots.**

LISTENING EXERCISE 3. 📀

LISTEN TO THE FOLLOWING WORDS CONTAINING ئـ AND REPEAT. LOOK AND LISTEN FOR THE KASRA OR ي IMMEDIATELY PRECEDING OR FOLLOWING HAMZA.

طائِرة   عائشة   خائِب   قائِل   أسْئِلة   قارِئ   طوارِئ

Now practice writing and reading ئـ by copying and sounding out these words:

شاطِئ   قَبائِل   طائِرات   سُئِلَ   رَئيس

ؤ

همزة على كُرسي الواو

When neither kasra nor ي precedes or follows hamza, if there is instead a ضمّـة or long vowel و, the hamza is written on a و seat: ؤ.

LISTENING EXERCISE 4. 📀

LISTEN TO THE FOLLOWING WORDS CONTAINING ؤ AND REPEAT. NOTICE THE DAMMA AND/OR و ON EITHER SIDE OF IT:

يُؤْسِف   بُؤْس   رَؤوف   رُؤوس   سُؤال   فُؤاد

Practice writing and reading ؤ by copying and sounding out these words:

يُؤَثِّر   أَصْدِقاؤُك   مُؤْلِم   تَفاؤُل

In other cases, that is, when medial همزة is surrounded by fatHa or alif, it is written on alif, as you learned earlier, **except** when it follows alif, in which case it rests on the line and takes no كرسي. (You can remember this by noting that Arabic does not allow two alifs to be written together.) You do not need to learn all the rules for writing hamza right away; for now concentrate on recognizing these five seats of hamza when you see them and learning to pronounce and write correctly words containing hamza one by one.

Vocabulary

LISTEN TO AND LEARN THESE WORDS AND EXPRESSIONS:

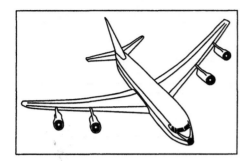

I have a question.	عندي سُؤال
How do we say..?	كَيفَ نَقول؟
I don't know.	لا أعرِف

طائِرة

DRILL 2.

YOU WILL HEAR ONE WORD OF THE THREE IN EACH ROW. CIRCLE THE ONE YOU HEAR:

ذعر	زار	زأر	١ـ
فزع	قرع	فرع	٢ـ
قلاب	كلاب	غلاب	٣ـ
ثورة	سورة	صورة	٤ـ
عرق	عرك	عرف	٥ـ
عائب	غائب	خائب	٦ـ
تفاءل	تفاعل	تفاؤل	٧ـ
شعل	سأل	سعل	٨ـ
ضباب	كباب	قباب	٩ـ
شاعر	ثائر	سائر	١٠ـ
زر	صر	سر	١١ـ
جبس	كبس	قبس	١٢ـ

Drill 3. DVD

CONNECT THE LETTERS TO FORM WORDS, THEN LISTEN AND WRITE THE VOWELS YOU HEAR:

ــــــــــــــــــ	=	ت + س + ا + ؤ + ل	١-
ــــــــــــــــــ	=	ظ + ر + و + ف + ي	٢-
ــــــــــــــــــ	=	و + ظ + ي + ف + ة	٣-
ــــــــــــــــــ	=	أ + ك + ل + ا + ت	٤-
ــــــــــــــــــ	=	غ + ر + ا + ئ + ب	٥-
ــــــــــــــــــ	=	ج + ح + ا + ف + ل	٦-
ــــــــــــــــــ	=	ف + و + ا + ئ + د	٧-
ــــــــــــــــــ	=	إ + ف + ر + ي + ق + ي + ا	٨-
ــــــــــــــــــ	=	خ + ل + ي + ف + ة	٩-
ــــــــــــــــــ	=	ض + ر + و + ر + ا + ت	١٠-
ــــــــــــــــــ	=	أ + ظ + ا + ف + ر + ي	١١-
ــــــــــــــــــ	=	أ + ن + هـ + ا + ر	١٢-
ــــــــــــــــــ	=	ك + ر + ي + م	١٣-
ــــــــــــــــــ	=	م + ذ + ا + هـ + ب	١٤-
ــــــــــــــــــ	=	ط + م + ا + ط + م	١٥-
ــــــــــــــــــ	=	ن + هـ + ا + ي + ا + ت	١٦-
ــــــــــــــــــ	=	ك + ل + ا + م + هـ	١٧-
ــــــــــــــــــ	=	أ + أ + ك + ل + هـ + ا	١٨-
ــــــــــــــــــ	=	ك + هـ + ر + ب + ا + ء	١٩-
ــــــــــــــــــ	=	ت + ع + ظ + ي + م	٢٠-
ــــــــــــــــــ	=	غ + ف + ر + ا + ن	٢١-
ــــــــــــــــــ	=	أ + س + ئ + ل + ة	٢٢-

DRILL 4.

READ THE FOLLOWING NAMES OF ARAB AND OTHER MIDDLE EASTERN COUNTRIES ALOUD, THEN IDENTIFY THEIR LOCATION ON THE MAP AND WRITE THE NUMBER THAT CORRESPONDS TO THE LOCATION OF EACH.

مِصْر ــــــ ــــــ   الجَزائِر ــــــ ــــــ   عُمان ــــــ ــــــ

سوريا ــــــ ــــــ   العِراق ــــــ ــــــ   تـونِس ــــــ ــــــ

السّودان ــــــ ــــــ   الأُردُن ــــــ ــــــ   لُبْنان ــــــ ــــــ

اليَمَن ــــــ ــــــ   قَـطَر ــــــ ــــــ   المَـغرِب ــــــ ــــــ

السّعوديّة ــــــ ــــــ   الإمارات ــــــ ــــــ   البَحْرَيْن ــــــ ــــــ

ليبْيا ــــــ ــــــ   الكُوَيْت ــــــ ــــــ   إسْرائيـل وفِلَسْطين ــــــ ــــــ

إيران ــــــ ــــــ   تُركيّا ــــــ ــــــ   موريتانيا ــــــ ــــــ

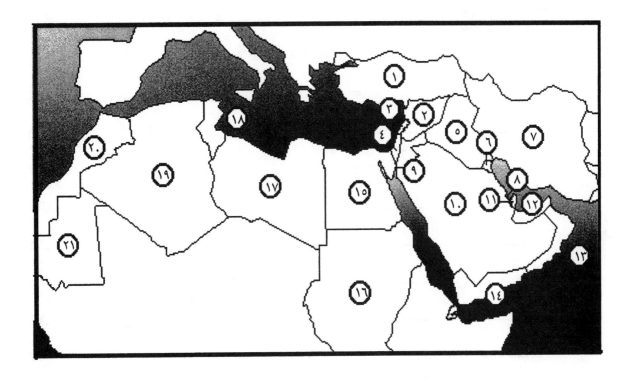

DRILL 5.

FIND A COPY OF AN ARABIC NEWSPAPER OR GO ONLINE TO FIND ONE. LOOK FOR WORDS YOU RECOGNIZE, SUCH AS NAMES, AND WRITE OUT TEN. THE FRONT PAGE IS A GOOD PLACE TO LOOK FOR NAMES OF PEOPLE AND PLACES IN THE NEWS.

Drill 6.

Following is a list of top business schools.

1. Find out:
   (A) whether your school is listed among them.
   (B) the top three schools.
   (C) the top three schools in your geographical area.

2. Using what you know about famous American colleges and universities, find and guess the meaning of these words:

(أ) كلية _____   (ب) معهد _____

افضل كليات التجارة وادارة الاعمال

المكانة العلمية	مجموع النقاط	درجة التصنيف / الجامعة
٢	١٠٠,٠	١- جامعة هارفارد
١	٩٧,٩	٢- جامعة ستانفورد
٢	٩٢,٧	٣- جامعة بنسلفانيا (معهد وارتون)
٢	٩١,١	٤- جامعة نورثويسترن (كيلوج)
٢	٨٩,٨	٥- معهد ماساتشوستس للتكنولوجيا (سلون)
٦	٨٧,٨	٦- جامعة شيكاجو
١١	٨٦,٠	٧- جامعة ديوك (فوكوا)
٧	٨٥,٦	٨- كلية دارتموث (تك)،
١١	٨٥,٤	٩- جامعة فيرجينا (داردن)
٧	٨٥,٢	١٠- جامعة ميشيجان
٧	٨٤,٥	١١- جامعة كولومبيا
١١	٨١,١	١٢- جامعة كورنيل (جونسون)
١١	٧٨,٥	١٣- جامعة كارنيجي ميلون
١٧	٧٨,٣	١٤- جامعة نورث كارولينا في تشابل هيل
٧	٧٧,٤	١٥- جامعة كاليفورنيا في بيركلي (هاس)
١١	٧٦,٧	١٦- جامعة كاليفورنيا في لوس آنجليس (اندرسون)
١٧	٧٦,٢	١٧- جامعة تكساس في أوستن
١٦	٧٦,١	١٨- جامعة انديانا في بلومينجتون
١٧	٧٤,٦	١٩- جامعة نيويورك (شتِرن)
٢٠	٧٣,٤	٢٠- جامعة بيردو في انديانا (كرانرت)
٢٥	٧١,٧	٢١- جامعة سوزين كاليفورنيا
٣٣	٦٨,٧	٢٢- جامعة بيتسبرج (كاتس)
٣٧	٦٨,٧	٢٣- جامعة جورجتاون
٣٣	٦٧,٧	٢٤- جامعة ماريلاند في كوليج بارك
٢٢	٦٧,٢	٢٥- جامعة روتشستر (سيمون) في نيويورك

من مجلة «المجلّة» ١٩٩١

Drill 7.

Get a map of your campus and label it in Arabic as much as you can to help any Arabic-speaking visitors to your school.

ARABIC SIGNS DVD
READ THE SIGNS ON THE DVD WITH YOUR TEACHER AND SOUND OUT AS MANY WORDS AS YOU CAN.

DIALOGUES DVD
WATCH SCENE 12 لازِم تِشرَبي حاجة! **WITH YOUR TEACHER.**

CULTURE: VISITING PEOPLE

Every culture has its own set of expectations and behaviors involving visiting. In Arab culture, hospitality is a highly prized virtue, and when you visit people at their home or workplace, they will generally insist that you at least have something to drink. The most common items offered are coffee, tea, and soft drinks. If you are invited for a meal, expect lots of food, for the hosts will go out of their way to serve you the most lavish meal they can. They will also keep piling food on your plate and insisting that you eat more! When you have had enough to eat, say الحَمدُ للّه .

You noticed in the video scene that when the host first offered a drink, the guest refused. The initial offer and refusal are somewhat formulaic in Arab culture, and are basically expressions of politeness on both sides. The guest refuses at first because he or she does not want to put the host out, and to show that he or she has not come just to have something to drink. A guest will often refuse several times before accepting.

When you are offered something, it is your responsibility as "offeree" not to impose too greatly. The offerer will go out of his or her way to be generous, but that is not an invitation for you to take advantage of the hospitality. Likewise, when you are entertaining visitors, remember to fulfill your role as host or hostess by insisting.

الوحدة العاشرة
UNIT TEN

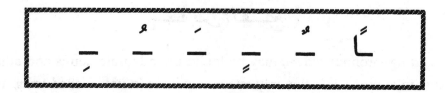

In this unit, you will learn about certain grammatical markers that are used in formal Arabic (not in everyday speech). These markers can occur on the ends of nouns and adjectives. You will hear and see them in formal speech, poetry, sacred texts, and children's stories and schoolbooks.

تَنْوين

The word *tanwiin*, derived from the name of the letter نون, refers to the *n* sound in these three endings:

ٍ (pronounced *in*)   ٌ (pronounced *un*)   ً (pronounced *an*)

The *n* sound is represented in writing by the doubling of the short vowel symbol. In formal Arabic, these endings occur on **indefinite** nouns and adjectives, and they indicate certain grammatical functions of words in a sentence. Except in very formal situations, such as public addresses, they are rarely used in speaking, and are only written in vowelled texts. They are for the most part superfluous to comprehension, since speech and normal prose rely on other grammatical devices, such as word order, to convey meaning. For the time being, you need not worry about their meanings; you are expected to recognize them simply as "grammatical endings" when you hear them.

Note that the ة *taa marbuuTa* is pronounced as ت before *tanwiin*, as you will hear in the following exercise.

LISTENING EXERCISE 1. 📀

LISTEN TO THE FOLLOWING WORDS BEING READ WITH EACH TANWIIN ENDING. WHETHER YOU HEAR AN, IN, OR UN, THE MEANING OF EACH OF THESE WORDS REMAINS THE SAME: A CAR, A MAN, AND A WOMAN.

امرأةٌ / امرأةً / امرأةٍ   رجلٌ / رجلاً / رجلٍ   سيّارةٌ / سيّارةً / سيّارةٍ

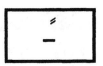

تَنْوِين الفَتْح

This ending, pronounced *an*, may be found on indefinite nouns and adjectives. Of the three tanwiin endings, it is the only one you will see in unvowelled texts, and the only one used in everyday speech, where it is found on certain expressions. You have already learned several words that end in تنوين الفتح.

LISTENING EXERCISE 2. 📀

LISTEN TO AND REPEAT THESE FAMILIAR WORDS THAT END IN تنوين الفتح, **NOTING THE SPELLING:**

أهلاً وسهلاً   أهلاً   مَرحَبًا   عَفوًا   شُكرًا

WRITING 📀

As you can see in the box above, تنوين الفتح has two different written forms. The form on the right, a double fatHa, is used on words that end in ة and اء (alif followed by hamza). The form on the left, in which تنوين الفتح rests on an alif seat, is used in most other cases. Compare the spelling of the words in row A to that of the words in row B:

A   ساعةً   استاذةً   مساءً   سماءً

B   شُكرًا   عَفوًا   جِدّاً   أهلاً

Like other short vowel markings, the double fatHa in تنوين الفتح is not normally written in unvocalized texts. **However, the alif seat that represents** تنوين الفتح **is always written where required,** which means that alif at the end of a word usually represents تنوين الفتح rather than a long vowel. Compare the vocalized words in row B above to the same words, unvocalized this time, in row C below:

C   شكرا   عفوا   جدا   اهلا

The function of final alif as a seat for تنوين الفتح may be easily distinguished from the vowel alif since, as you have learned, Arabic words do not usually end in alif because

the usual spelling for final long vowel alif is ى . Therefore, when you see an Arabic word that ends in alif, such as شكرا or أهلا , it is likely that the alif represents تنوين الفتح . Remember also that the sound *an* at the end of a word usually indicates تنوين الفتح , and is distinct in form and meaning from the human adjectival ending -ان that you hear on words like بردان and تعبان .

In fully vowelled texts, تنوين الفتح is written as a double fatHa when it occurs on ة or final ا ء . When it occurs on other letters, it is written as an alif with a double fatHa, which can rest either on top of or slightly in front of the alif, depending on the script or font used. Practice writing تنوين الفتح by copying the examples:

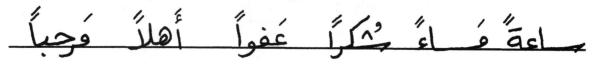

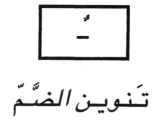

تَنوين الضَّم

This symbol is called تنوين الضَّم and is pronounced *un*. It represents a certain grammatical ending on indefinite nouns and adjectives. You will see or hear it only in fully vowelled texts and formal speeches.

LISTENING EXERCISE 3. 📀
LISTEN TO THE FOLLOWING EXAMPLES OF تنوين الضَّم **AND REPEAT:**

طالبٌ   ساعةٌ   قلمٌ   استاذةٌ   كتابٌ

WRITING 📀

Written تنوين الضم has two main variants, both of which are commonly used and signify the same sound and meaning. The chart shows, on the right, two Dammas, written close together, and on the left, a Damma with a hooked tail.

We will not be using تنوين الضم for some time, but you may see or hear it, so learn to recognize these as variants of this grammatical ending. Practice writing it by copying the examples:

كِتابٌ أُستاذةٌ قَلمٌ ساعةٌ طالبةٌ شُبّاكٌ

[ٍ]

تَنوين الكَسر

This symbol is called تنوين الكَسر, pronounced *in*. It represents the third and final grammatical ending that can occur on indefinite nouns and adjectives. Like تنوين الضم, it only appears in fully vocalized texts and formal contexts.

LISTENING EXERCISE 4. DVD
LISTEN TO THE FOLLOWING EXAMPLES OF تنوين الكسر **AND REPEAT:**

طالبٍ   ساعةٍ   قلمٍ   استاذةٍ   كتابٍ

WRITING DVD

When it is written in vowelled texts, تنوين الكسر is always written the same way: two kasras. Practice writing it by copying the examples:

كِتابٍ أُستاذةٍ قَلمٍ ساعةٍ طالبةٍ شُبّاكٍ

You will learn more about تنوين الكسر and تنوين الضم later, when you begin studying the case system of formal Arabic. For now, we will not use them, because they are not used in everyday speech, and informal Arabic does not rely on them to convey meaning. However, you will soon learn more about تنوين الفتح, which does appear in spoken Arabic in expressions such as شكراً and أهلاً وسهلاً.

The three تنوين endings, الفتح والضم والكسر, can occur only on **indefinite** nouns and adjectives. In addition, Arabic has three endings that occur on **definite** nouns

and adjectives, which correspond to the three short vowels, فَتحة , ضَمة , and كَسرة .
Like the indefinite تنوين endings, these grammatical endings are only used in formal
situations and are only written in vocalized texts. Thus, in a formal context, الطالب might
be pronounced or marked: الطالبُ or الطالبَ or الطالبِ , depending on the grammatical
role of الطالب in the sentence. However, since the grammatical role of the noun in question
will be clear from other sentence clues, these endings are usually superfluous to meaning.
The important thing for you to remember is that all three of these mean *the student*.

LISTENING EXERCISE 5. 📀

LISTEN TO THESE WORDS AND PHRASES READ WITH GRAMMATICAL ENDINGS فَتحة , ضَمّة , AND كَسرة:

الطالبِ	الطالبَ	١ـ الطالبُ
الاستاذةِ	الاستاذةَ	٢ـ الاستاذةُ
مدينةِ نيويورك	مدينةَ نيويورك	٣ـ مدينةُ نيويورك

You will only see these endings in fully vocalized texts, and only hear them in very
formal contexts. We will return to their meanings later; for now, just recognize them as
"grammatical endings" when you hear them.

DRILL 1. 📀

READ ALOUD THE FOLLOWING PHRASES, WRITTEN IN FORMAL ARABIC AND VOCALIZED:

٧ـ هذا رجلٌ طويل .

١ـ – أهلاً وَسَهلاً !
– أهلاً بك !

٨ـ هذهِ سيّارةٌ جميلة

٢ـ – نَعيماً !
– أنْعَمَ اللّهُ عَلَيْك !

٩ـ شاهَدتُ فيلماً فَرَنسيّاً أمس .

٣ـ – مَرحَبًا !
– مرحبًا بك !

١٠ـ أسْكُنُ في مَدينةٍ كبيرة .

٤ـ – شُكرًا !
– عَفوًا .

١١ـ اشتَرَيْتُ سيّارةً جديدة .

٥ـ الحَمدُ لِلّه !

١٢ـ اشتَرى الاستاذُ الكتابَ مِنَ المَكتَبة .

٦ـ هيَ في مدينةِ القاهرة .

Drill 2.

CIRCLE ALL OCCURRENCES OF ‏الـ‎ AND THE ENDING ‏اً‎ IN THE FOLLOWING ADVERTISEMENT. ALSO IDENTIFY ALL THE WORDS AND NAMES YOU CAN:

(‏من جريدة الشرق الاوسط ١٩٩٢‎)

وسواء اخترت السفر على الدرجة الأولى، أو درجة رجال الأعمال، أو الدرجة السياحية، فإنك ستسافر في جو من الراحة والرفاهية حيث تستمتع بكرم ضيافتنا الأصيلة.

كل هذا جزء من تجربة الطيران، بأسلوب طيران الخليج الرفيع.

الآن، طيران الخليج توفر لكم رحلات أسبوعياً الى فرانكفورت وامستردام كل يوم اثنين وجمعة مروراً بالبحرين، وكل سبت مروراً بالدوحة. المسافرون من السعودية يمكنهم السفر على هذه الرحلات الى فرانكفورت الساعة ٦،٠٥ صباحاً وامستردام الساعة ٨،١٠ صباحاً.

GULF AIR

طيران الخليج

- 146 -

Writing One-Letter Particles

Particles and prepositions that consist of only one letter are written **connected to the following word**. The most common of these are:

and	و
for, belong to (indicates *possession*)	لـِ
with/in (indicates *instrument*)	بـِ

Remember: لـ and بـ are connecting letters and so are attached to the following word. Since the letter و does not connect, **it must be written close to the following word, and should never be left "stranded" at the end of a line.** Practice joining words with و by copying the following, and note that Arabic uses و as we would use a comma to link items together in a list:

مصر ولبنان وسوريا وتونس والعراق

_____

_____

When the preposition لـ is written with a word beginning with الـ , **the alif is elided** to streamline the form of the word. For example, to say *belonging to the student*, we need to write preposition لـ with the noun الطالب . To do that, we first drop the alif of الـ and write preposition لـ connected to the لـ of الطالب like this: للطالب . Remember this rule:

لـِ + الـ ← لـِ لـ

Drill 3.

Practice connecting و , لـ , and بـ in the following phrases and figure out their meaning:

٦ـ لـ + الأستاذ _____		١ـ انا + و + انت _____	
٧ـ بـ + الكمبيوتر _____		٢ـ بـ + الإنجليزية _____	
٨ـ بـ + السيارة _____		٣ـ لـ + الدكتور _____	
٩ـ لـ + البنت _____		٤ـ بـ + العربية _____	
١٠ـ لـ + الولد _____		٥ـ و + حضرتك؟ _____	

JUSTIFICATION OF MARGINS

In type or print, margins may be justified or evened by lengthening the connecting segment between letters. This may be done between any two connecting letters; it does not affect the reading of the word at all. For example, الكتاب may be written: الكـــتـاب or الكتـــــاب . Do not confuse this lengthening, which occurs only in **print**, with that of toothless ـس (ـــ), which occurs only in **handwriting**.

DRILL 4.
CIRCLE ALL EXAMPLES OF MARGIN JUSTIFICATION YOU CAN FIND IN THE FOLLOWING POEM:

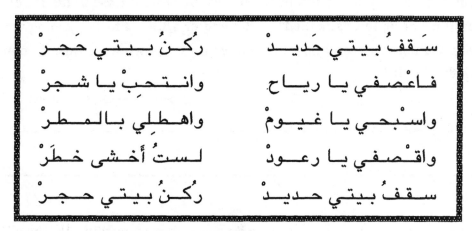

من قصيدة «الطمأنينة» للشاعر اللبناني ميخائيل نعيمة

HANDWRITING

As you have been learning throughout this workbook, Arabic handwriting exhibits some variations from the printed form. In addition, handwriting itself varies according to both regional and individual style. For example, the teeth of ـس and ـش are normally written in North African handwriting.

The biggest variation you will find in the shape of the letters will be in the word-final shapes. In Egypt, for example, the letters ض , ـق and ـن are sometimes written without their dots and given a hook on the end of their tails instead when they occur in word-final position. Another letter that shows word-final variation is ـة . Take a look these examples:

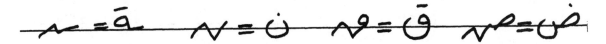

With practice, you will gradually learn to recognize various handwriting styles and conventions. Look at various styles you come across, and imitate the ones you like best as you develop your own style.

DRILL 5.

READ AS MUCH AS YOU CAN OF THE FOLLOWING HANDWRITING SAMPLES. LOOK FOR FAMILIAR WORDS AND TRY TO GUESS NEW ONES FROM CONTEXT. WHAT OBSERVATIONS CAN YOU MAKE ABOUT THE VARIATION OF LETTERS IN HANDWRITING STYLES? AFTER READING, WRITE A SIMILAR PASSAGE PROVIDING INFORMATION ABOUT YOURSELF.

Sample I:

> أهلاً وسهلاً ومرحباً !
> اسمي جورج اسطفان وانا من مدينة بيروت في
> لبنان . أسكن في شارع "باريس"، وأنا استاذ
> في الجامعة اللبنانية . عندي ٢ أولاد .

Sample II:

> بسم الله الرحمن الرحيم
> اسمي سناء مصطفى . أنا مصرية من القاهرة .
> اسكن في الزمالك في شارع ٢٦ يوليو . أنا
> طالبة في جامعة القاهرة .

Sample III:

> أهلاً وسهلاً
> إسمي غادة منصور وأنا من مدينة طرطوس في
> سوريا . مدينتي على البحر وهي قريبة جداً من
> لبنان . زوجي من مدينة بصير في حوران .

ARABIC SIGNS DVD
READ THE SIGNS ON THE DVD WITH YOUR TEACHER AND SOUND OUT AS MANY WORDS AS YOU CAN.

CULTURE: THE DEVELOPMENT OF THE ARABIC WRITING SYSTEM

The Arabic writing system is believed to have evolved from the Aramaic script through the Nabateans, Arab tribes living to the north of the Arabian Peninsula (present-day Jordan) in pre-Islamic times. This early version of Arabic script survives in inscriptions dating back to the third and fourth centuries A.D., which represent the earliest known of many stages of development. Although writing was known in the Arabian Peninsula before Islam, it was the early Muslims who developed the script that we know today, in order to preserve the text of the Quran by putting it down in writing. Tradition holds that the first compilation of the Quran was recorded during the reign of عُثمان, the third Caliph (d. A.D. 656). Even then, though, the script was not complete, for surviving fragments show text devoid of short vowel markings and dots, as the following sample shows:

«روح الخط العربي»، تأليف كامل البابا، دار العلم للملايين، بيروت ١٩٨٨

The addition of short vowel signs began during the reign of Ali (علي), the fourth Caliph (d. A.D. 661), and the dots that distinguish between letters of similar shape were added during Umayyad rule, around the end of the seventh century. Further development of the individual shapes of letters occurred at the beginning of the Abbasid period (from A.D. 750).

CALLIGRAPHY 📀

Calligraphy is a highly developed art form. Since the time of the earliest script form you saw above, called Kufic, artists have continuously developed new styles and designs. Quranic verses, poetry, and proverbs written in intricate scripts often adorn books, monuments, and public buildings. Professional calligraphers combine form and meaning by working Quranic verses into pictures such that the letters and dots form a design. Below are four artistic renderings of the phrase

(*In the Name of God the Merciful and Compassionate*)   بِسم الله الرَّحمن الرَّحيم

See how many letters you can pick out in each sample:

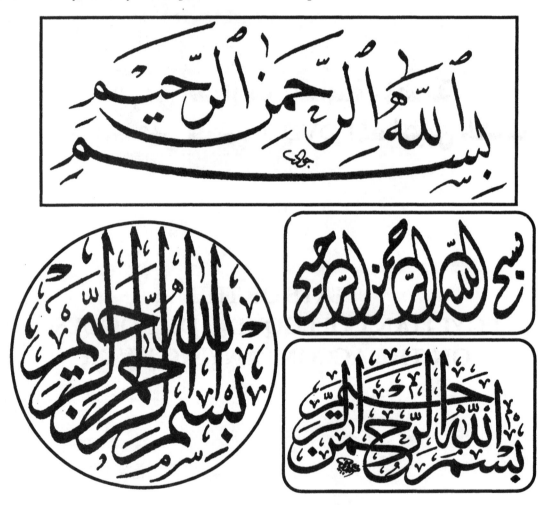

ON YOUR DVD, WATCH USTAAZ EL-SHINNAWI WRITE THE WORDS ألف باء AND اللـغـة العـربيـة IN VARIOUS CALLIGRAPHIC STYLES, LOOK AT OTHER SAMPLES OF ARABIC CALLIGRAPHY, AND VISIT AN ARABIC CALLIGRAPHER IN HIS SHOP IN CAIRO.

★ تمّ بحمد الله ★

APPENDIX

نصوص الحوارات بالعامية المصرية
المسجلة على قرصي الـ DVD المصاحبين للكتاب

TEXTS OF THE
EGYPTIAN COLLOQUIAL DIALOGUES
ON THE ACCOMPANYING DVDS

UNIT ONE

أهلاً وسَهلاً !

- ❖ أهلاً وسَهلاً ومَرحَباً بِكُم! اسمي حُسني بنّيس ، وأنا من المَغرِب من مَدينة مِكناس .

- ❖ السّلامُ عليكُم ! أنا اسمي عُلا نَجاح الشّالجي . أنا من مدينة بغداد في العِراق .

- ❖ صَباح الخير ! أنا اسمي شُكري جوهَر ، وأنا من مِصر من مدينة القاهرة .

- ❖ صَباح الخير ! أنا اسمي إكرام المَصمودي . أنا من تونِس من مدينة صفاقِس .

- ❖ أهلاً وسَهلاً ! أنا اسمي وَفاء أبو النّعاج ، فَلسطينيّة من مدينة النّاصِرة .

- ❖ السّلامُ عليكُم ! أنا اسمي عَوَض مُبارك من السّودان ، وفي السّودان أنا من مدينة الخُرطوم كيف حالكُم ؟

UNIT TWO

حَضرِتِك من مَصر؟

عماد : أهلاً وسَهلاً .

سامية : أهلاً بيك .

عماد : اسمي عِماد , واسم حَضرتِك ؟

سامية : اسمي سامية .

عماد : تَشَرّفنا , حَضرتِك من مَصر ؟

سامية : أيوه من مصر .

عماد : أهلاً وسهلاً .

سامية : أهلاً بيك , وحَضرتَك ؟

عماد : أنا من الإسكندِريّــة .

سامية : أهلاً وسهلاً .

عماد : أهلاً بيكِ .

UNIT THREE

SCENE THREE المشهد الثالث

ازّيّ حَضرتِك ؟

د. زينَب :	صَباح الخير يا سامية .
سامية :	صَباح النّور يا دُكتورة زينب , ازّيّ حضرتِك ؟
د. زينب :	الحَمدُ لله . ازّيِّـك انتِ ؟
سامية :	الحمد لله .

SCENE FOUR المشهد الرابع

صَباح الخير !

شريف :	صباح الخير يا عِماد .
عماد :	أهلاً , صباح النّور يا شريف , ازّيّك ؟
شريف :	الحمد لله , وانتَ , ازّيّك ؟
عماد :	الحمد لله , أخبارك إيه ؟
شريف :	تَمام , الحمد لله , وانتَ ؟
عماد :	الحمد لله !

UNIT FOUR

SCENE FIVE المشهد الخامس

اِزّيّك؟

شريف :	أهلاً يا دكتور عبّاس .
د. عباس :	أهلاً يا شريف ، اتفَضَّـلوا !
شريف :	شُكراً . ازّيّ حضرتَك ؟
د. عباس :	الحَمد لله , ازّيّك انتَ ؟
شريف :	الحمد لله . إبراهيم , صاحبي , طالب فى جامعة القاهرة
د. عباس :	تَشرّفنا .
إبراهيم :	تشرّفنا بيك .

المشهد السادس   SCENE SIX

الحمد لله

سامية :	صباح الخير يا دُعاء .
دعاء :	صباح النور يا سامية ,ازيك ؟
سامية :	الحمد لله , ازيك أنتِ ؟
دعاء :	كويّسة , الحمد لله .
سامية :	أمينة ، صاحبتي , طالبة في الجامعة الأمريكية .
دعاء :	أهلاً وسهلاً .
أمينة :	أهلاً بحضرتِك .

UNIT FIVE

المشهد السابع   SCENE SEVEN

تَشَرَّفنا

د.عبّاس :	اتفضّل!
دعاء :	مَساء الخير يا دكتور عباس .
د. عباس :	مساء النور يا أستاذة دعاء , اتفَضَّــلي . ازيّك ؟
دعاء :	الحمد لله . ازيّ حضرتَك ؟
د. عباس :	الحمد لله . الدكتور مَحمود البطل , الأستاذة دعاء سعيد
د. محمود :	أهلاً وسهلاً , تشرفنا .
دعاء :	أهلاً بيك . حضرتك أستاذ في الجامعة الأمريكية ؟
د. محمود :	لأ , في الحقيقة أنا أستاذ فى جامعة ايموري في أمريكا
دعاء :	أهلاً وسهلاً .
د. محمود :	أهلاً وسهلاً بحضرتِك .

طَيِّب , اِتفَضَّلي !

أهلاً يا سامية .	دعاء :
أهلاً يا دعاء . ازَيِّك ؟ أخبارِك إيه ؟	سامية :
تَمام , الحمد لله , ازَيِّـك أنتِ ؟	دعاء :
الحمد لله .	سامية :
طَب عَن إذنِك , عندي فَصل .	دعاء :
طَيِّب , اتفضَّلي , مع السَّلامة .	سامية :
الله يِسَـلِّمِك .	دعاء :

يَلا !

صباح الخير يا شريف .	عماد :
صباح النور يا عماد , ازَيِّك ؟	شريف :
الحمد لله , أخبارك إيه ؟	عماد :
تَمام , الحمد لله .	شريف :
تِشرَب قهوة ؟	عماد :
آه والله .	شريف :
طَيِّب , يَلا بينا !	عماد :
يَلا .	شريف :

SCENE TEN المشهد العاشر

ألو !

+ : ألو .

- : ألو ، حضرِتَك الدُّكتورة زينَب لُطفي ؟

+ : لا يا افَندِم ، النِّمرة غَلَط .

- : طَب ، أنا آسفة .

+ : لا مَعليهش , مع السَّلامة .

UNIT EIGHT

المشهد الحادي عشر   SCENE ELEVEN

سَلامْتِك

الصديقة :   مالِك يا سامية ؟

سامية :   تَعبانة شوَيّة .

الصديقة :   سَلامْتِك .

سامية :   الله يِسَلِّمِك .

UNIT NINE

المشهد الثاني عشر   SCENE TWELVE

لازِم تِشرَبي حاجة !

د. عباس :   مَعَ السّلامِة يا أستاذ تامِر .

تامر :   الله يسلّمَك .

دعاء :   صباح الخير يا دكتور عباس .

د. عباس :   صباح النور يا أستاذة دعاء . اتفضّلي , أهلاً وسهلاً .

دعاء :   شكراً , ازّيّ حضرتَك ؟

د. عباس :   الحمد لله , ازّيّك انتِ ؟

دعاء :   كوَيِّسة ,الحمد لله .

د. عباس: تِشربَي قَهوة ؟

دعاء :   لا , شُكراً .

د. عباس: لأ , لازِم تشربي حاجة .

دعاء :   لأ, ولا حاجة .

د. عباس: شاي ولا قهوة ؟

دعاء: طَيِّب ...قهوة .

قاموس إنجليزي- عربي

English-Arabic Glossary

A

address	عُنْوان
airplane	طائِرة
Algeria	الجَزائِر
and	وَ
angry	زَعلان / زَعلانة
Arab, Arabic	عَرَبي / عَرَبيّة
astonishing, strange	عَجيب / عَجيبة
at, in [location in space and time]	في
automobile, car	سَيّارة

B

beautiful, pretty	جَميل / جَميلة
belonging to, for	لِ
big, large	كَبير / كَبيرة
book	كِتاب
bookstore, library	مَكْتَبة
boy	وَلَد
bread	خُبْز
pita bread	خُبْز عَرَبي
brother	أخ
building	بِناية
bus	أوتوبيس / باص
but	لـٰكِن

C

car, automobile	سَيّارة
chair	كُرسي

chicken	دَجاج
city	مَدينة
class, classroom	فَصْل ؛ صَفّ
clock, watch	ساعة
close, nearby	قَريب / قَريبة
coffee	قَهْوة
Arabic coffee	قَهْوة عَرَبيّة
American coffee	قَهْوة أَمْريكيَّة
cold (adjective: feeling cold)	بَرْدان / بَرْدانة

D

darling, dear (to a female)	حَبيبَتي
darling, dear (to a male)	حَبيبي
daughter, girl	بِنْت
desk, office	مَكْتَب
difficult, hard	صَعْب / صَعبة
distant, far	بَعيد / بَعيدة
doctor (M.D., Ph.D.)	دُكتور / دُكْتورة
door	باب
drill	تَمْرين

E

easy	سَهْل / سَهْلة
Egypt	مِصْر
evening	مَساء
examination, test	اِمْتِحان
excuse me	عَن إذنَك (تفَضّل / تفَضّلي :reply)

exercise, drill	تَمْرين
exhausted	خَلْصان / خَلْصانة

F

far, distant	بَعيد / بَعيدة
fine, good	كوَيِّس / كوَيِّسة
five	خَمْسة
for, belonging to	لِ
four	أرْبَعة
friend	صاحِب / صاحِبة
friends	أصْحاب
from	مِن

G

get well soon!	سَلامتَك! (الله يِسَلِّمَك reply)
girl, daughter	بِنْت
go: I go to	أذْهَب إلى
God	اللّه
expression used when praising someone	ما شاءَ اللّه !
God willing	إنْ شاءَ اللّه
in the name of God	بِسْم اللّه
may God have mercy on him	اللّه يِرْحَمُه
there is no god but God	لا إله إلاّ اللّه
good, fine	جَيِّد / جَيِّدة ؛ كوَيِّس / كوَيِّسة
good-hearted (for people) / good, tasty (for food)	طَيِّب / طَيِّبة
good evening	مَساء الخَير — مَساء النّور (reply)
good morning	صَباح الخَير — صَباح النّور (reply)
good bye	مَعَ السَّلامة — اللّه يِسَلّمك (reply)

H

happy	سَعيد / سَعيدة
hard, difficult	صَعْب / صَعْبة
have: I have	عِنْدي
he	هُوَ
hello, hi	أهْلاً (وَسَهْلاً) — أهْلاً بِك (reply)
	السَّلامُ عَلَيْكُم — وَعَلَيْكُمُ السَّلام (reply)
	مَرحَبًا — أهْلاً / مَرحبتَـيْن (reply)
homework	واجِب
hot (feeling hot)	حَرّان / حَرّانة
house, home	بَيْت
how ?	كَيْفَ ؟
how are you?	ازَّيَّك ؟ / كَيْفَ الحال ؟
hungry	جَوْعان / جَوْعانة

I

I	أنا
I have	عِنْدي
in	في
Iran	إيران
Iraq	العِراق
Israel	إسرائيل

J

Jordan	الأُردُن

K

kind (person)	طَيِّب / طَيِّبة
know: I know	أعْرِف
I don't know	لا أعْرِف
Kuwait	الكُوَيْت

L

large, big	كَبير / كَبيرة
Lebanon	لُبْنان
lesson	دَرْس
library, bookstore	مَكْتَبة
Libya	ليبيا

M

man	رَجُلْ
Mauritania	موريتانيا
milk	حَليب
Miss	آنِسة
Mr.	سَيِّد
Mrs.	سَيِّدة / مَدام
money (feminine)	فُلُوس
morning	صَباح
good morning	صَباح الخَير — صَباح النّور (reply)
Morocco	المَغرِب

N

| name | اِسْم |
| nearby, close | قَريب / قريبة |

neighbor	جار / جارة
never mind , that's OK	مَعْلِهش (مَعْليش)
new	جَديد / جَديدة
news	أخبار
nice (of people)	لَطيف / لَطيفة
nine	تِسْعة
no	لا
notebook	دَفْتَر
number	رَقَم
zero	صِفِر (٠)
one	واحِد (١)
two	اِثْنان (٢)
three	ثَلاثة (٣)
four	أرْبَعة (٤)
five	خَمْسة (٥)
six	سِتّة (٦)
seven	سَبْعة (٧)
eight	ثَمانية (٨)
nine	تِسْعة (٩)
ten	عَشَرة (١٠)

(O)

office, desk	مَكْتَب
OK, fine	طَيِّب !
Oman	عُمان
on (top of)	عَلى
one	واحِد

P

page	صَفْحة
Palestine	فِلَسْطين
paper (leaf of)	وَرَقة
pen, pencil	قَلَم
please (to a female)	مِنْ فَضْلِك
please (to a male)	مِن فَضْلَك
please (come in / go ahead / sit down)	تفَضَّل / تفَضَّلي
pretty, beautiful	جَميل / جَميلة
professor	أُستاذ / أُستاذة
professors	أَساتِذة

Q

Qatar	قَطَر
question	سُؤال
I have a question	عِنْدي سُؤال
The Quran	القُرآَن

R

room	غُرْفة

S

sad , upset	زَعْلان / زَعْلانة
Saudi Arabia	السَّعوديّة
say: we say	نَقول
how do we say ?	كَيْفَ نَقول ؟
she	هِيَ
short	قَصير / قَصيرة
sick	مَريض / مَريضة

sister	أُخْت
small	صَغير / صَغيرة
spacious, wide	واسِع / واسِعة
story	قِصّة
strange, odd	غَريب ، عَجيب
street	شارِع
student	طالِب / طالِبة
Sudan	السُّودان
sugar	سُكَّر
Syria	سوريًا

T

table	طاوِلة
tall	طَويل / طَويلة
tasty, good (food)	طَيِّب / طَيِّبة
tea	شاي
teacher	أُسْتاذ / أُسْتاذة
telephone	تَليفون
test / examination	اِمْتِحان
thank you	عَفْوًا (reply شُكْرًا)
thank God	الحَمْدُ لِلّه
thirsty	عَطْشان / عَطْشانة
this (feminine)	هـٰذِهِ
this (masculine)	هـٰذا
tired	تَعْبان / تَعْبانة
to (motion toward)	إلى
Tunisia	تونِس

U

United Arab Emirates الإمارات

upset زَعلان / زَعلانة

W

watch, clock ساعة

water ماء

weird, strange غَريب عَجيب

welcome أهلاً وَسَهْلاً — أهلاً وَسَهْلاً بك (reply)

wide / spacious واسِع / واسِعة

window شُبّاك

with [people] مَع

with [things; instrumental] بِـ

woman اِمْرَأة

word كَلِمة

Y

Yemen اليَمَن

yes نَعَم / أيْوه

you (feminine) أنْتِ

you (masculine) أنْتَ

you (feminine, polite) حَضْرِتِك

you (masculine, polite) حَضْرِتَك

young people, "guys' شَباب

Z

zero صِفِر

COMPONENTS OF THE *AL-KITAAB* LANGUAGE PROGRAM

Alif Baa

Alif Baa with Multimedia: Introduction to Arabic Letters and Sounds
Second Edition
ISBN 978-1-58901-506-7, paperback with 1 CD-ROM bound in
(All audio and video materials combined on CD-ROM)

Answer Key to Alif Baa
Second Edition
ISBN 978-1-58901-036-9, paperback

....

Part One

Al-Kitaab fii Ta^{c}allum al-^{c}Arabiyya with DVDs
A Textbook for Beginning Arabic, Part One
Second Edition
ISBN 978-1-58901-104-5, paperback with 3 DVDs bound in
(All audio and video materials combined on DVD)

Answer Key to Al-Kitaab, Part One
Second Edition
ISBN 978-1-58901-037-6, paperback

....

Part Two

Al-Kitaab fii Ta^{c}allum al-^{c}Arabiyya with DVDs
A Textbook for Arabic, Part Two
Second Edition
ISBN 978-1-58901-096-3, paperback with 3 DVDs bound in
(All audio and video materials combined on DVD)

Answer Key to Al-Kitaab, Part Two
Second Edition
ISBN 978-1-58901-097-0, paperback

....

Part Three

Al-Kitaab fii Ta^{c}allum al-^{c}Arabiyya with DVD and MP3 CD
A Textbook for Arabic, Part Three
With New Video Material!
ISBN 978-1-58901-149-6, paperback with DVD and MP3 CD bound in

....

Audio On the Go
These CDs contain MP3 files of the audio only from the Alif Baa and Al-Kitaab volumes. Perfect for those students who want the portability of MP3 files for practice, these files can be transferred to an MP3 device, played on a computer, or played on some home CD players.

Alif Baa Audio On the Go ISBN 978-1-58901-152-6
Al-Kitaab Part One Audio On the Go ISBN 978-1-58901-150-2
Al-Kitaab Part Two Audio On the Go ISBN 978-1-58901-151-9

For price and ordering information, visit our website at www.press.georgetown.edu or call 800-537-5487.
For more information on teaching the *Al-Kitaab* language program, visit www.alkitaabtextbook.net.